Building Towers,
Forming Gardens

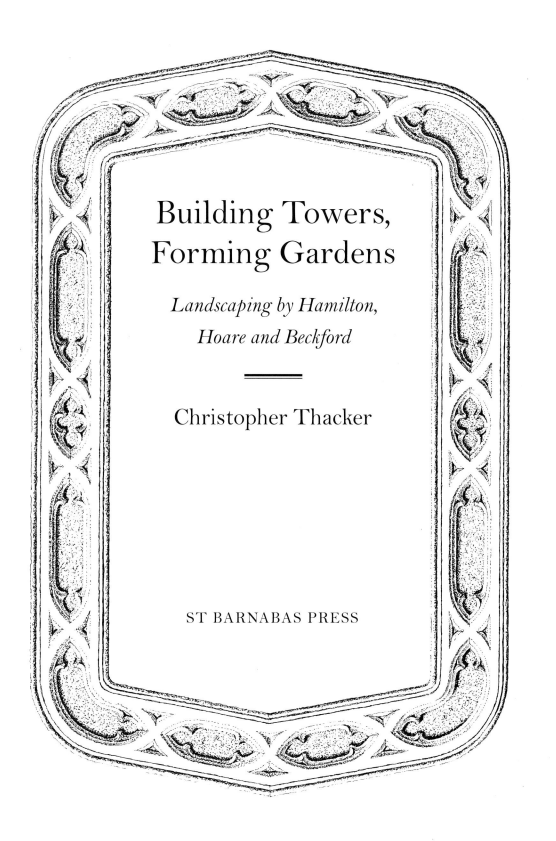

Building Towers, Forming Gardens

Landscaping by Hamilton, Hoare and Beckford

———

Christopher Thacker

ST BARNABAS PRESS

Author's Note

This small volume began in my mind after Julian Berry had
asked me to help with the 'garden part' of the William Beckford
Exhibition in 1976 – for me a happy task, leading to the
garden chapter for the catalogue, and then to my little book on
Joseph and Josiah Lane, *Masters of the Grotto.*
My thanks to Julian Berry for encouraging me in these matters
are deep and considerable; and I should also acknowledge
the generous advice of Mavis Collier, of the
Painshill Park Trust. Thank you!

© Christopher Thacker 2002

Wood engraved vignettes by Richard Shirley Smith

Designed by Humphrey Stone

Printed by BAS Printers Ltd
Over Wallop, Stockbridge, Hants

ISBN 0-9508213-2-2

Published by the St Barnabas Press
2 Dover House Road, London SW15 5AU

Contents

Introduction

William Beckford (1760–1844), named by Byron and then by himself as 'England's wealthiest son', was a garden enthusiast beyond most of our wildest dreams. This we shall talk about in the main part of this book. But his inspirations, his ideas, his garden and landscape passions came both from two other garden-lovers, Charles Hamilton (1704–86) and Henry Hoare (1705–85), and the gardens they created, at Painshill and at Stourhead. The complex connections between these three men – and their garden-creations – are so important that it is indeed necessary to write a little – if not a lot! – about Hamilton and Painshill, Henry Hoare and Stourhead, as a proper prelude to writing about Beckford and Fonthill. Nor must we forget the work of Alderman Beckford (William Beckford's father, 1709–70, whom, to avoid confusion, we shall call the Alderman in this text) in 'landscaping' much of the Fonthill property before William Beckford was born . . .

These three gardens were begun within a few years of each other – Painshill, in Surrey, in 1738 or soon after; Fonthill, in Wiltshire, in the 1740s, and Stourhead, also in Wiltshire, and nine miles or so westward from Fonthill, in 1743 or 1744.

Hamilton, the Alderman and Hoare were all amateur garden-makers, taking a serious part in deciding the layout and ornamentation of their gardens. They were 'gentleman gardeners', having, or fondly hoping to have, money enough to hire professionals to complete, and to execute, the schemes which they had in mind. The Alderman was without doubt the wealthiest of the three, and at the same time the most committed to his political activities in London. His own part in the direction of his gardens appears to have been much less than that of Hamilton or Hoare, whose long, personal involvement with their gardens gave to each a separate and distinctive character.

All three went to the same school, Westminster; Hamilton in 1718, Hoare one or two years later, and the Alderman in January 1718/19. Hamilton and the Alderman then went on to Oxford, graduating in 1723 and 1729 respectively.

All three continued their education with one or more visits to the continent, and it is almost certain that all three, at different periods, visited Florence, Rome, and possibly Naples.

Links such as these are not uncommon among educated and well-to-do contemporaries in the 18th century. But for these three people they were much strengthened when, in the early 1740s, the Alderman acquired his estate at Fonthill, and so became a country neighbour of Henry Hoare at Stourhead, nine miles away; soon after, he acquired an additional estate at Witham, less than two miles north of Stourhead. Then, in 1747, Charles Hamilton opened an account at Hoare's Bank, and in March borrowed £6000 on mortgage, which was required to repay part of a loan from his friend Henry Fox – money he had borrowed for his garden improvements; and in 1756, the Alderman married Maria Marsh, who was Charles Hamilton's niece.

They knew each other, they were connected in many ways, they visited each other's property occasionally, and gardens were a topic which they discussed, and about which there was an element of emulation, even of rivalry. One further, and fascinating, link appears in their periodic employment of Joseph and Josiah Lane (father and son), talented builders – and designers – of grottoes in all three gardens.

Coming to the next generation, these connections continued to influence the final, immense development of Fonthill by William Beckford, the Alderman's son.

I

'The Patriarch of Modern Gardening'

'I know of no event but the death of Mr. Charles Hamilton, one of my patriarchs of modern gardening', wrote Horace Walpole to Lady Ossory on 28 September 1786. Walpole's appelation is right – just as Walpole himself was, by then, the grand old man of the Gothic style. Walpole had been one of the first to comment on Hamilton's work at Painshill, when he had written to George Montagu on 11 August 1748 'I have been to see Mr Hamilton's near Cobham, where he has really made a fine place out of a most cursed hill'. On that occasion, Walpole had almost certainly visited Painshill in company with Thomas Gray. He was to repeat the visit in 1761, and possibly to go at least once more in the 1760s, to arrive at the high opinion of Hamilton and Painshill which appears in his essay *On Modern Gardening*, published in 1771.

But in 1748 Hamilton was still no more than a decade into his great work, which had begun, as Walpole said, from a 'most cursed hill'. He began more or less from scratch, having some 200 acres by the mid-1740s – mostly forming a single area, running east-west for about a mile, and bordered on the lower, southern and eastern side by the winding course of the River Mole. When he came, there was probably no existing garden, certainly no park, and no mansion, only a 'very small' house.

The earliest reference to his work is in the 1742 edition of Defoe's *Tour thro' the Whole Island of Great Britain*, III, 293–7. This is part of an appendix added by Defoe's successor, probably Samuel Richardson.

Defoe had died in 1731. It catches Hamilton in the very first stages, so often forgotten in descriptions of a completed scheme:

> At Painshill . . . is a great Improvement making by inclosing a large Tract of Land designed for a Park, which was most of it so poor as not to produce any thing but Heath and Broom; but by burning of the Heath, and spreading of the Ashes on the Ground, a Crop of Turneps was obtained; and by feeding Sheep on the Turneps, their Dung became a good Manure to the Land, so that a good Sward of Grass is now upon the Land, where it was judged by most People impossibole to get any Herbage.

The writer digresses to talk of the public utility of this sort of 'improvement', then praises the 'fine Inequalities' of the Painshill estate:

> for every 100 yards there are great Hollows, then rising Grounds again, so that the Prospect is continually changing, as you walk over it; and (if we may guess by what this Gentleman has already done) the Whole will be laid out conformable to the natural Situation of the Ground; and when the Plantations, which are already made, are grown up, it will be a delightful place; and this upon a Spot of Ground, which lay almost neglected, before this Gentleman became possessed of it.

In other words, Hamilton's 'park' is still a-making in 1742. No architectural features are mentioned, nor the lake, so that we may assume that work on these had not begun. Hamilton is still at the first, and most arduous stage. It is likely that, while he may always have envisaged a landscaped park 'conformable to the natural Situation of the Ground', with its 'fine Inequalities', his relatively modest means forced him to go carefully.

Hamilton's own ambitions, theories and feelings about the aesthetic quality of Painshill are largely unknown. He wrote no books, and few of his letters survive. We depend on the comments of visitors, who seem to have formed their views without guidance from the owner. Joseph Spence, who had no doubt spoken with him about the making of Painshill, is tantalisingly brief on the theory – Hamilton 'directed and over-saw all the operations, both in the buildings and gardens' (*Observations*, ed. J. M. Osborn, 2v., 1966, item 1103).

In contrast, what we know from Hamilton himself is concerned with practice. Two accounts by Hamilton survive, to do with the making of the lawns, and with his vineyards, which were both part of his first garden development.

On lawns, he wrote to Lord Kildare in the 1760s (*Holland House Papers*, British Library, Add. MS 51408, ff. 152–3), explaining in detail the several years' cleaning, ploughing and harrowing, and varied sowings, necessary to establish a sweep of grass (then kept short by sheep). For his vineyards he had special pride. He established two vineyards at Painshill, one in the south-eastern corner of the property, of about 5 acres, and another of 5 to 10 acres in a detached part of his estate, north of the Cobham road. The first was laid out fairly early in his programme, being well-established by 1748, when a Huguenot émigré, David Geneste, was taken on to improve the vineyard, and to lay out the second area in the following year.

The climate in southern England was not always favourable to vine-growing at that period, but Hamilton persevered, and was obviously proud of his product. Near the end of his time at Painshill, he wrote a detailed account of his work, which was included in Sir Edward Barry's *Observations . . . on the Wines of the Ancients*, 1775, pp. 471–6. His methods responded to the uncertainty of the climate – after a poor start with red wine, he changed to white, which he sweetened by 'putting three pounds of white sugar-candy to some of the hogsheads'. He explains this as

'A Scene in the Gardens of Pains Hill' – the lake, with the Gothic pavilion beyond
(S. Wale, in R. Dodsley, *London and its Environs Described*, 1761)

being 'in order to conform to a rage that prevailed, to drink none but very sweet Champaign'.

Yet the yield was generally slight, and – though he once sold 'five hundred pounds worth at one time' – it did not solve his financial problems.

South of the vineyard, and running east-west for several hundred yards, was the lake, the largest single feature in Hamilton's landscape. Not mentioned in Defoe's *Tour* of 1742, it was made in two stages, the first in the mid-1740s, and the second – an extension to the east, below the vineyard – not until *c.*1770. The main islands lay roughly midway along the completed lake. It was wholly artificial, being set in an area of excavated ground running beside, yet above, the course of the River Mole. No stream fed it from above, the water being pumped up from the river, twelve or fifteen feet below. The water-wheel-pump, activated by the flow of the river, which turned it round like a paddle-wheel, was remarked on by several visitors, who all say that Hamilton designed it. Pococke's words – 1754 – are clear enough: 'It consists of four spiral square pipes from the radius to the center, the mouth being open; it conveys the water to the axel where 'tis emptied, and the water is convey'd by pipes to the [lake]'. This pump has recently been re-created on the original site, as a part of the restoration of Hamilton's gardens by the Painshill Park Trust.

One more of Hamilton's practical devices should be mentioned – the use of rope netting, proofed with pitch, to enclose his shrubberies and young trees, and protect them from the several hundred sheep which grazed the lawns. So: lawns, vineyards, lake and pump, and netting round the shrubberies – these are all described in practical terms which would be uncommon in the letters of a wealthy gardener – at Stourhead or Fonthill such references are virtually unknown. And they are, with one exception, the first to be executed. Thus far, Charles Hamilton was proceeding with a degree of caution. His garden buildings are still some years ahead.

There is one other early element of the gardens which may not have been so prudently conceived. When in 1742 Defoe's *Tour* refers to the 'Plantations, which are already made', there is nothing to suggest that these are other than trees or shrubs of a nondescript kind. But by the 1750s, their distinctive character is remarked. Not only are they laid out in a new way – 'naturally' – but they are themselves unusual. Robert FitzGerald (mid-1750s) writes:

The Naturale Inequality of the Ground make's it Naturally pleasing . . . adorn'd with Noble trees irregularly scatter'd intermix'd with an Infinity of flowering Shrubs and Evergreens, flocks of sheep feeding up and down, a Noble piece of water which looks Naturale tho not so . . . this is the Nearest Nature of any fine improvement I have seen the Walks are the Naturale sod (in M. Symes, 'Robert FitzGerald's tour of Surrey gardens', *Journal of Garden History*, VI, 4, October – December 1986, 323).

Pococke, in 1754, has a different emphasis. The kinds of trees are indicated more clearly: There is a 'small lawn encompassed with evergreens, and leading to the greenhouse'; there is 'the Botanical walk, in which there are evergreens of all kinds . . . They have all sorts of pines and firr trees in this place, particularly the Jerzey firr or pine, and they have much of the Virginia acacia as well as cedar'.

'The Botanical walk' indeed – Hamilton was soon be renowned for his adventurous plantings of rare trees, and by 'about 1781' Charles von Linné, son of the great Linnaeus, 'asserted, that a greater variety of the fir was to be found here, than at any other spot in the world which he had ever seen' (in J. P. Neale, *Views*, 2nd series, v. I, 1824).

The later accounts of the size, variety and excellence of the Painshill conifers are in a sense a reflection of Hamilton's unusual enthusiasm in the middle years of the century. By 1786 Thomas Jefferson could remark 'there is too much evergreen' – the growth of the trees was spectacular – and in 1803 D. B. Lambert, in *The Genus Pinus*, and J. C. Loudon in 1838, in the *Arboretum & Fruticetum Britannicum*, write with high praise of Hamilton's fervour in introducing new trees and shrubs.

Hamilton was noted for this in his own time. He corresponded in the mid-50s with the Abbé Nolin in Paris, and in 1766 the Scottish botanist, Dr John Hope, included Painshill among his visits round London (see J. H. Harvey, 'A Scottish Botanist in London', *Garden History*, IX, 1, 1981, 62). It has therefore been possible to draw up lists of the trees and shrubs which Hamilton grew, from which the re-stocking of appropriate areas of the grounds at Painshill has been undertaken in recent years – see M. Symes, 'Charles Hamilton's Plantings at Painshill', *Garden History*, XI, 2, 1983, 112–24, and Mark Laird, *The Flowering of the Landscape Garden*, 1999, pp. 3-18.

Important too was the use which Hamilton's friends made of him – as an adviser for their own garden improvements. Normally it seems to have been in connection with garden design, and the creation of isolated features, but in the 1750s at Holland Park in Kensington (for his old friend Henry Fox) he may have advised on tree planting as well.

* * *

By the mid-1750s Hamilton had therefore achieved a great deal: he had cleared the heath, turning it to lawns and walks, planted with a great variety of trees and shrubs. There were two vineyards. He had created a lake, with islands; and the whole was admired for its exceptional planting and for the 'naturalness' of its scenic effects. As Mrs Elizabeth Montagu wrote in July 1755,

> It beggars all description, the art of hiding art is here in such sweet perfection, that Mr. Hamilton cheats himself of praise, you thank Nature for all you see, tho' I am inform'd all has been reformed by Art (in Elizabeth Montagu . . . *Correspondence*, ed. E. J. Climenson, 2v., 1906, II, 76).

Hamilton's achievement was indeed to be admired – yet it was extraordinary as well. In the known references to Painshill between the late 1730s, when he began, and 1760, there is virtually nothing said about garden buildings – let alone a new house – appropriate to the scale of his gardens. Pococke in 1754 mentions a 'greenhouse', and several visitors refer to his ingenious water-wheel. In the south-east corner of the estate, there was a kitchen garden with walls, discreetly screened from the main 'landscape'. Of other garden buildings, not a word. A straightforward explanation is the age-old complaint, identified by Panurge as faute d'argent.

Then, in 1760–61, there is sudden and copious evidence of garden buildings – so copious, that we may assume that some had been there for two or three years, and were part of a scheme which Hamilton had decided to carry out. He wrote to Henry Fox on 25 May 1761 of 'all the buildings I have erected within these three years . . . and by this time twelve months I shall have put up all the buildings I would wish to have here, all that ought to be here' (in Norman & Beryl Kitz, *Pains Hill Park*, 1984, p. 71). It is certain that by 1763, all the features known to have been built at Painshill were in existence, with the exception of the enlargement of the grotto, the ruined abbey, and the eastern extension of the lake. Both the grotto enlargement and the ruined abbey must have been conceived in conjunction with the plan to extend the lake, since its presence, beside and round the abbey and the grotto, defines their positions in the landscape.

Suddenly, as I have said, the garden buildings are there – a mixed collection. An engraving by William Woollett, published in 1760, shows a view across the lake, with two bridges, the Turkish tent, the mausoleum, and, in the distance, the Gothic tower or belvedere. Crossing the lake is a boat, driven by a paddle-wheel, cranked by an energetic servant. The next year, visitors confirm some of these features, and add to the list the rock-work cascade, at the west end of the lake, the ten-sided Gothic pavilion, and the temple of Bacchus. By 1763 the hermitage has been built, there is a sculptured group of the Sabine Women, and work on the grotto has almost certainly begun – this last was ready by 1767, and then extended in 1770, while the ruined abbey was built in 1772. The eastern arm of the lake must have been filled last of all (it does not appear on Gilpin's sketch plan of 1772), presumably in 1773 or soon after.

The temple of Bacchus (William Gilpin, August 1772).
Courtesy of Mrs George Benson

It is an impressive list, and visitors were duly impressed. The architectural features appear to have been designed mainly by Hamilton himself. Spence's statement that he 'directed and oversaw all the operations' is not much upset by the discovery that Robert Adam produced designs for the interior of the temple of Bacchus, or that Henry Keene designed the Turkish Tent (see N. Kitz, *op. cit.*, pp. 64–6.). The grotto is also likely to have been the work of Joseph Lane of Tisbury (see my *Masters of the Grotto: Joseph and Josiah Lane*, 1976, pp.10–12.), but closely directed by Hamilton.

The Gothic tower or belvedere (William Gilpin, August 1772).
Courtesy of Mrs George Benson

Though mixed in style, these buildings did not clash with one another, as the grounds were extremely varied, thanks to Hamilton's two decades of landscaping and planting. The different areas allowed to each building its distinctive atmosphere.

It is clear that his gardens were planned as an entity, set in the curving, gently or steeply sloping grounds above the River Mole, with the long lake winding along the bottom of the slope; in some areas, the view outwards was important, as from the temple of Bacchus, in others, the view inwards or across the gardens was what mattered – as from the Gothic pavilion. From the Turkish tent, the 'best' view was obtained, both outwards – to the south, beyond the Mole – and across the gardens. This, it should be remembered, was the spot he had chosen to build his mansion, when the right moment arrived. In the temple of Bacchus he kept his best pieces of sculpture, with the 'noble Bacchus', some seven feet tall. 'Would not part with it for its weight in gold – the best on this side of the Alps', he said to Spence – not once, but 'twice or thrice'.

When, in 1773, he sold Painshill, the Bacchus was included in the sale, but in 1797 (11 years after his death) when Painshill and its contents again came on the market, his great-nephew William Beckford bought the statue for £400, and in 1800–01 it was noted as the main ornament of the dining-room at Fonthill Splendens.

The Gothic tower – or belvedere – stood near the far west boundary. Hamilton probably built it as an 'eye-catcher', a suggestion of the feudal past, brooding over the idealised landscape. In Woollett's engraving of 1760 it is a small object on the horizon, just one part of the grand view; yet it was – and is – the tallest of Hamilton's garden buildings, four-sided, with a battlemented top and a slim conical turret at one corner. Gilpin's sketch in 1772 gives it a stronger presence, and today it may be admired, magnificently restored, as one passes along the A3 road from London to Portsmouth. Its importance stretches far beyond the boundaries of Painshill, for by 1762 it had been seen by Henry Hoare of Stourhead, prompting him to build the far greater edifice of Alfred's Tower – which led in turn to the Alderman beginning another even larger tower at Fonthill, on a site which his son, William, would consider for his first tall, embattled tower in the 1790s.

* * *

The grotto may have been 'a whimsical little object' when it was first seen by Gilpin in 1765. By then, it was still two years old at the most,

The interior of the grotto (Elias Martin, *c*.1770).
Courtesy of the National Museum, Stockholm

and Hamilton had it enlarged around 1770. When complete, it was extensive, and must have been extraordinary, both from the outside, and within. Though the roof of the main chamber fell in after the Second World War, the remaining walls and arches are still impressive, and the several drawings made by 18th-century visitors – Gilpin in 1772, Elias Martin in the 1770s, and Frederick Piper, who made a detailed plan in 1779 or 1780 – record a complex and exciting structure, which is now being splendidly restored.

Hamilton is thought to have had a guiding hand in the design, while Joseph Lane of Tisbury probably saw to the construction. Most of it was on one island in the lake, being only a little above the level of the water, and with delightful glimpses outwards across the surface of the lake. On one side a massive arch connects the grotto-island to an adjacent island, forming at one and the same time a bridge between the two islands, and a tunnel under which visitors' boats may be paddled. The islands were planted with cedars, robinia and laurel. While the structure was essentially built of bricks, roofed over with beams and slates, the cave-like appearance was achieved by covering the visible parts of the grotto with a layer of limestone (on the outer sides) and with plaster inside, covered when damp with a variety of hard, crystalline materials – quartz, gypsum, calcite, coral, fluorite and cinders. The irregular limestone blocks on the 'outer' sides (for example, within the tunnel-bridge between the islands) are pierced with deep, round holes – like flatulent gruyère – and were then known as 'pierre antidiluvienne' since its water-worn appearance suggested immense age, as if in a cave washed by the sea since before the Flood. Here above all I regret the absence of comment by Hamilton himself. What did he think of it? What visits, parties, or gentle solitary hours, happened here in his time?

The hermitage has gone. But its importance at Painshill was as great as that of any other feature. It was set in the thickest and darkest part of the hanging wood of conifers – 'encompassed with thicket, and over-hung with shade' (T. Whately, *Observations on Modern Gardening*, 1770, p. 187). Backed against the sloping ground, it was 'formed to the front with trunks of fir trees with their bark on, their branches making natural Gothic windows' (Parnell), 'the cell . . . composed of logs and roots' (Whately). It had one room at the back – 'the poor hermit's dark bed-chamber' (Spence), with 'a little straw couch, an old table and a few old chairs' (Parnell). We may appreciate these comments when we know that Hamilton is supposed to have hired someone to act the part of a hermit in this building. Later embroideries on this matter are piquant but unsubstantiated, alleging a 7-year contract, for 700 guineas, in which period the hermit was to have no contact with barber, beer or barmaid.

The hermitage (William Gilpin, August 1772).
Courtesy of Mrs George Benson

While other tame hermits are known to have been hired at this time – at Hawkstone in Shropshire, for example – or to have offered themselves for hire (see my *The Wildness Pleases*, 1983, pp.127–129), Hamilton's proceedings remain open to speculation. While doubting that he could ever imagine affording 700 guineas for such an unshaven luxury, I fancy he might have drafted one of his vignerons to fill the post in an emergency. With or without a hermit, the hermitage and its setting received high praise:

I mean that kind of Alpine scene, composed almost entirely of pines and firs, a few birch, and such trees as assimilate with a sav-

The ruined abbey, with the hermitage on the wooded slope beyond
(William Gilpin, August 1772). Courtesy of Mrs George Benson

age and mountainous country . . . Mr. Hamilton has given a perfect example of this mode . . . all is great and foreign and rude; the walks seem not designed, but cut through the wood of pines' (Horace Walpole, *On Modern Gardening*, in *Anecdotes of Painting in England*, 3v., 1876, III, 87–8).

Later in the century such places were to be among the deepest inspirations for the garden projects of young William Beckford – so central, that we might imagine Fonthill Abbey to be no more than a gigantic 'hermitage'.

To return for a moment to Painshill. Hamilton's gardens had no declared theme, no political or artistic 'signposts' for visitors to read and follow. Of course there were walks, their direction guided in part by the lake. But there was no set itinerary, and there were no thoughtful inscriptions on urns, pedestals or monuments (as there were, for example, at Stowe, or the Leasowes) to give one political or poetical guidance. For Hamilton, it seems, the merit of his garden lay in its 'naturalness', not in any more learned message. John Wilkes, friend of Boswell, ally of the Alderman, put it well, writing to his daughter on 9 June 1772: 'I sauntered through the elysium of Mr. Hamilton's gardens till eight in the evening, like the first solitary man through Paradise (*Correspondence of John Wilkes*, 5v., 1805, IV, 102).

*   *   *

But the money had run out. From 1770 onwards, Hamilton had been making efforts to sell first his sculptures, and then the estate. On 5 Oct. 1771 John Wesley had found Painshill 'inexpressibly pleasant', but added 'And now, after spending his life in bringing it to perfection, the grey-headed owner advertises it to be sold! Is there anything under the sun that can satisfy a spirit made for God?' (Wesley, *Journal*, ed. N. Curnock, 8v., 1909–16, V, 431-2). In April 1773, Painshill was sold. Hamilton moved to London, and then, in July 1773, to 14, Royal Crescent, Bath.

There he married again, in 1774, and gardened again, and the young William Beckford, his great-nephew, visited him twice, the second time most certainly with gardens in mind. In July 1781 Beckford wrote

> My mother urges me without ceasing to visit our holy uncle in Bath, the everlasting C- H-, who it seems, is building a house to his garden and adding peach house to grape house and pinery to pinery on the slope of the crescent hill which is already more than half

embroidered with his vagaries (in L. Melville, *Life and Letters of William Beckford*, 1910, 116).

'The everlasting C- H-' is Walpole's 'patriarch of modern gardening'. Nothing remains of Hamilton's garden work at Bath. But Hamilton's long-lasting contacts with other garden makers continued until his death in 1786.

II

'A Charming Gaspard Picture'

Four or five years after Charles Hamilton started gardening at Painshill, Henry Hoare began to create his paradise at Stourhead. His father, Henry Hoare I (1677–1725) had acquired the manor of Stourton in 1718, and though he had built a new Palladian house, designed by Colen Campbell, he set only a small area of garden round it. His widow, who lived at Stourhead until her death in 1741, does not appear to have added any significant feature apart from a 'fir walk' to the west of the house, running roughly north-south along high ground between the house and the present lake. The obelisk (1746) was to be sited at the northern end of this walk. Their son, the second Henry Hoare, went to live at Stourhead in 1741, and began to develop the extensive area of valleys and surrounding slopes to the west and south-west of his father's house from 1743–44 onwards. He was therefore beginning from scratch, as Charles Hamilton had done, and as his near neighbour in Wiltshire, Alderman William Beckford, was to do at Fonthill from the late 1740s onwards.

While Hamilton's estate was bounded by the River Mole, and Alderman Beckford's was crossed by the Fonthill stream, Henry Hoare's property at Stourhead enclosed the several sources of the River Stour which, until his time, fed a group of fishponds descending in a roughly north-to-south direction. Three of these, the most elevated, still survive in their early 18th-century form.

Like Charles Hamilton, Henry Hoare was himself the designer of his gardens, though it is likely that Hamilton's work at Painshill, and Hamilton's discussions with Henry Hoare, played a noteworthy part in the creation of Stourhead.

Unlike Hamilton, however, Henry Hoare was a man of ample and continuing means. He had travelled abroad, mainly in Italy, in the 1730s, and like Hamilton he had collected works of art. When it came to garden-making, Henry Hoare was able to employ architects, artists and craftsmen on a scale far beyond Hamilton's means. His principal garden buildings, erected over some thirty years, are of a solidity and grandeur which bear comparison with the grandest buildings at Blenheim, Castle Howard or Stowe.

Though Henry Hoare lived at Stourhead from 1741 onwards, when not in London, his development of the gardens did not begin in earnest until 1743 or 1744. In his study of the life and work of Henry Hoare and Richard Colt Hoare at Stourhead, *Landscape and Antiquity* (1970), Kenneth Woodbridge has indicated the strong element of moral seriousness in Henry Hoare's character. His attitudes colour both the process of garden-making, and the nature of the gardens themselves, and in so doing separate him to some extent from Charles Hamilton, financially insecure, yet incurably smitten with the *furor hortensis*, and from the plutocratic, impatient, good-hearted yet vulgar Alderman Beckford. Henry Hoare's moral stance appears most succinctly in a letter of 30 January 1755 to his nephew Richard Hoare, who was about to marry Henry Hoare's younger daughter Anne (quoted in Woodbridge, *op. cit.*, p. 42). Gardens such as Stourhead are 'the fruits of industry and application to Business' – while the objects within the gardens and their enjoyment, 'Temples, Grottos, Bridges, Rocks, Exotick Pines [e.g. pineapples] and Ice in Summer' must remain 'the envy of the indolent'. Only 'the industrious' have the 'best claim' to these delights, 'provided their foundation is laid by the hand of prudence and supported by the perseverance in well-doing and constant cautious watchfulness . . .'

So serious a view goes far to explain the careful, far-reaching plan for the gardens at Stourhead which he initiated in 1743–44, and which was more or less completed by the mid-1750s – the central lake, held in by a sizeable dam, being made in 1754–55. The plan involved the building of temples and a grotto, all with classical associations, round a lake to be formed from several of the existing ponds in the valley area west and south-west of the house. I say 'plan' (though no statement or document to this effect from Henry Hoare exists) since the three main buildings – the temple of Ceres (later named the temple of Flora), the temple of Hercules (later named the Pantheon) and the grotto – were all sited and built, or well under way, before the lake was made from the southern fishponds. Already present in this scheme was the village church, St Peter's, downhill and southwards from the house, and some distance inland and eastwards from the intended lake. Linking the buildings round the lake were grassed walks, like Hamilton's at Painshill, and the slopes of the valleys were planted mainly with beech and fir – unlike Hamilton's great and adventurous variety of unusual trees and shrubs.

Notably absent from this landscape was the house itself, hidden by rising ground. From the house, views stretch out over parkland from the north-west to north, north-east, east and south-east. The house still remains wholly invisible from the gardens.

The architectural features in this first plan seem to have been designed by Henry Flitcroft (1697–1769), with guidance from Henry Hoare, and adorned with sculpture by various artists. Walking round the lake – anti-clockwise, and first to the north-west – one would have reached a wooden bridge crossing the northern tip. This bridge was mistakenly thought by some to be 'Chinese', but others saw (or were told by their guide) that it was 'Palladian'. It was in fact taken from book III of Palladio's *Four Books of Architecture*, illustrated both in Leoni's version (1715) and in that of Isaac Ware (1738), and is of importance when discussing Hamilton's connection with Stourhead. Richard Colt Hoare had it taken down in 1798.

Passing along the western shore, the grotto was reached, low down by the water's edge. Designed by Flitcroft, and built 1744–48, possibly with the (subordinate) help of Joseph Lane, its original form was, we may say, 'regular', with a domed central chamber, flanked by lesser areas to left and right, looking out over the lake. The view out includes the temple of Flora and the village church. In the central chamber is the statue of a sleeping nymph (attributed to Cheere), with lines by Alexander Pope:

> Nymph of the grot these sacred springs I keep
> And to the murmur of these waters sleep . . .

In the further room is the statue of a river god (by Cheere). From the grotto, steps rise up to the grassy walk round the lake, and to a new scene hidden from the grotto by a spur of rising ground. The temple of Hercules, or Pantheon, was designed by Flitcroft, and its construction went on from 1753 until 1761.

The lake, planned from the start as the centre of the landscape, was not developed until 1754–55. To raise the level of the water to unite the several ponds in the valley, a sizeable dam was necessary to the south-west, and this was made in 1754. The transformation effected by the creation of the lake is well described in two accounts, by Dr Richard Pococke in 1754, and by Jonas Hanway in 1755. Whereas accounts of Painshill and of Fonthill, written in the same years, describe gardens which are to a large extent complete, the Stourhead gardens are seen as much as a future intention as a present achievement. Having passed the – completed – temple of Flora, Pococke writes (*Travels*, II, 43) that 'below this are two large pieces of water which are to be made into one

The Pantheon, seen across the lake
(William Gilpin, in *Observations on the Western Parts
of England*, 1798)

and much enlarged for which a head [or dam] is making at great expence'.

The developments in this lake come next: 'There are to be three islands in it, with different kinds of buildings in them, one of which is to be a Mosque with a Minaret.'

Then he describes the grotto, which is complete, and passes to the temple of Hercules, or Pantheon, 'not yet finished', for which a 'Colossal Statue of Hercules' by Rysbrack 'is making in London'. No other writer ever mentions buildings on the small islands – let alone a 'Mosque with a Minaret'.

A year later, Hanway's account reveals the gardens in delightful completion, ready to be enjoyed:

[33]

'Several irregular walks of different breadths' lead into the valley, where 'there is a very large piece of water at the bottom, on which there is a very pretty boat. You will remember it the longer by the female rower, whose vivacity induced her to try her skills . . . We made a coasting voyage on the little enchanting ocean, where we discovered several little islands, which are either planted or covered with rocks, uninhabited except by the feathered kind' (Jonas Hanway, *A Journal of Eight Days Journey from Portsmouth to Kingston upon Thames*, 2v., 1755, I, 138).

No mosque, no minaret. Instead, the completed lake is now crossed near the northern tip 'by a light wooden bridge of one arch . . .'. This bridge was to remain until 1798, when it was removed. A more costly, more beautiful replacement was built near the eastern end of the lake in 1762. Both bridges, from different designs by Palladio, are discussed below.

Hanway then describes the grotto and the Pantheon. Then, in his last paragraph, he proclaims the perfection of the gardens. The landscape is harmonious, an 'august and captivating scene'. His approval of the unity of the gardens is characteristic of his heavily moral attitude throughout the *Journal*:

Here we ought to contemplate not only what delights, but what does not shock. In this delicious abode there are no Chinese works; no monsters of imagination; no deviations from nature, under the fond notion of fashion or taste: all is grand, or simple, or a beautiful mixture of both (Hanway, *op. cit.*, I, 142).

That was in 1755.

*   *   *

Until 1762 or thereabouts, the Stourhead landscape conceived by Henry Hoare was therefore simple, grand and coherent, with a few well-spaced buildings of classical or renaissance-classical inspiration. It was once suggested that this landscape, with its walk round the lake, passing each building in turn, and with varied views at each point of the other features, was planned as a 'programme', with deliberate reference to the theme of Aeneas, his heroic trials, journeyings and eventual foundation of Rome. I prefer to think that Henry Hoare's intention was far less specific, and much more to do with a general wish that his gardens should resemble an idealised classical landscape, rich in poetic and artistic allusions – a form of paradise. In my experience of gardens, old or new, there is an astonishing rapport (though Henry Hoare could not possibly have known this!) between the house-less walk round the Stourhead landscape – at no point does the residence appear – and the Japanese concept of the 'stroll garden', where – as at the 17th-century garden of Shugaku-in, outside Kyoto – one may walk round the water-features and small related buildings, looking inwards and across the garden, and outwards to the landscape, without being aware of the Imperial residence.

It is important to note that Henry Hoare does not seem to have left any statement that the walk round his gardens had what we might now call a 'message' or a 'programme'; nor do any of his visitors remark on this either. Since the lake is central to the gardens their route tends to go round it; but even this is begun from different points, and may also be varied by taking a boat.

The 'message' at Stourhead was subtle, and delicately conveyed. Having left the house behind them, hidden by hill-slope and trees, visitors were indeed presented with 'a charming Gaspard picture' (Henry Hoare's phrase in 1762), or, elsewhere, with echoes of paintings by Claude, and with promptings of the excellence, worth and beauty of the antique world. The whole scheme is set in a spacious, 'natural' landscape of lake, springs, lawns and thickly wooded slopes. The most valuable contemporary comment is, I think, that of Horace Walpole (who visited Stourhead in 1762), in his essay *On Modern Gardening*, written *c.*1770. Here, discussing Milton's description of Eden, Walpole claims that Milton has foreseen the landscape gardens of the 18th century, and adds:

> The description of Eden is a warmer and more just picture of the present style than Claude Lorrain could have painted from Hagley or Stourhead. The first lines I shall quote exhibit Stourhead on a more magnificent scale.
>
> 'Thro' Eden went a river large,
> Nor changed his course, but thro' the shaggy hill
> Pass'd underneath ingulph'd, for God had thrown
> That garden as his garden-mound, high rais'd
> Upon the rapid current' (*Paradise Lost*, IV, 222).

Not Claude, not Gaspard, nor the story of Aeneas, but, as Henry Hoare himself wrote to his nephew Richard Hoare in Jan.1755, 'the enchanting paths of paradise' (in Woodbridge, *L. & A.*, p.30).

* * *

By October 1762 change was in the air. Henry Hoare had been to see Charles Hamilton's gardens at Painshill, with their new and varied buildings, and this, with other less certain inducements, moved him to 'improve' his own gardens. He wrote on 23 Oct.1762 to his daughter of the new 'Stone bridge of 5 arches' which was 'now about' at the eastern tip of the lake, and which would, with the view of the village church beyond, make 'a charming Gaspd picture' (in Woodbridge, *L.& A.*, pp.

The Roman bridge and the Pantheon, by Sir Richard Colt Hoare
(in J. Britton, *The Beauties of Wiltshire*, II, 1801)

52–53). The bridge was modelled on one by Palladio, and – apart from adding a genuine 'Italian' touch to the scene, reminiscent of Gaspard or Claude – gave emphasis to the eastern view. It is variously called the Palladian, the Roman, or even the Turf bridge, from the grass laid over the stone paving.

Two more classical features were still to be added. When in 1757 Robert Wood had published his *Ruins of Balbec and Palmyra*, Henry Hoare had promptly bought a copy, and the idea of Stourhead's temple of Apollo, modelled on the temple of the sun at Baalbec, may go back to that year. Whether Henry Hoare previously thought to build a temple on the site, on the high ground south of the lake, and south of the public road, we do not know. The actual temple of Apollo at Stourhead, designed by Flitcroft, was built between 1765 and 1767, and a rocky arch from the gardens over the public road, and a tunnel back under the road in the direction of the Roman bridge were both made in the early 1760s to allow undisturbed access to this additional garden area.

In its splendid way the temple of Apollo is as much a commemoration of a recent, and important event (in this case, the re-discovery, recording and delineation of ancient ruins) as the monument to Captain Cook at Stowe (erected in 1778), or the small, but still impressive replica of the iron bridge at Ironbridge in Shropshire which was built in 1791 in Fürst Franz von Anhalt-Dessau's gardens at Wörlitz.

So far, these additions are of a classical kind. But in his letter of 23 October 1762, Henry Hoare goes on to outline another project, 'one Scheme more which will Crown or Top all', which marks a fundamental change in direction. He is writing about Alfred's Tower, designed by Flitcroft, but not far advanced until the late 1760s, and completed only in 1772, three years after Flitcroft's death.

To 'Crown or Top all'? At Stourhead, Alfred's Tower is now known only to the more determined visitor. More or less invisible from the gardens, owing to the dense growth of woodland trees, its distance from the lake and encircling walks leaves it outside today's hurried itineraries. But to Henry Hoare the importance of this tower was genuine, and its size and situation were to provoke emulation at nearby Fonthill in 1769–70. Not only was Henry Hoare 'outdoing' Hamilton's Gothic tower at Painshill, but he was erecting a British landmark high above his secluded Stourhead estate.

The idea – related to the Saxon (and 'Gothic') inheritance of the British people – had already been 'in the air' at Stourhead for a little while. In December 1761, the poet-gardener William Shenstone refers to a poem which a friend had sent him, which had been 'planned . . . in Mr. HOARE'S lovely grounds at Stourton, and the Thought suggested by surveying, from an Eminence, a woody Vale, wherein ALFRED is reported to have once concealed himself from the Danes' (William

Shenstone, *Letters*, ed. M. Williams, 1939, p.612). Henry Hoare wrote in his letter of 23 October 1762 that he had been prompted to raise a memorial to King Alfred from reading praise of him in Voltaire's *Essai sur les moeurs*, but his first architectural scheme was not a Gothic one – he wrote 'I intend to build it on the plan of St Mark's Tower at Venice'.

The project was however allowed to rest, and when in the mid-1760s Flitcroft drew up the design which was eventually executed, it was – like Hamilton's tower, but far taller – in the Gothic idiom. Unlike the Painshill tower (and indeed unlike St Mark's in Venice!) it was given a triangular plan. It has a round turret at each corner, a battlemented parapet, and stands some 160' high. A part of the long inscription reads 'Alfred the Great / A.D. 879 on this summit / Erected his standard against the Danish Invaders / . . . / The Father of his People / The Founder of the English / Monarchy and Liberty'.

Further encouragement towards the 'Gothic' had come in June 1763, when Henry Hoare visited Strawberry Hill, Horace Walpole's Gothic creation at Twickenham. Henry Hoare was clearly impressed by the recently-completed Great Gallery and the adjacent vaulted Cabinet – it was 'most exquisite . . . a Sanctum Sanctorum and tho Gothick dissolves the scene in Extasy' (quoted in Woodbridge, *L.& A.*, p.59). We might note that Walpole's visit to Stourhead, written up in detail in his *Visits to Country Seats*, was in July 1762, and that the two enthusiasts must surely have discussed gardens on these occasions.

Gothic too, like Alfred's Tower, was the Bristol High Cross, erected at Stourhead in 1765 between the Roman Bridge of 1762 and St. Peter's church, and so completing the 'charming Gaspard picture'. The monument had first stood in Bristol at the crossing of High Street and Broad Street, and was eventually transported to Stourhead in 1764.

The last important addition to the gardens in Henry Hoare's time was the hermitage, first mentioned by Henry Hoare himself in November 1771: 'I am building a Hermitage . . . It is to be lined inside and out with old Gouty nobbly oakes, the Bark on' (quoted in Woodbridge, *L.& A.*, pp.61–62).

*   *   *

While Henry Hoare's own originality in designing these gardens is undisputed, it is just as certain that he was aware of other designers, and garden enthusiasts, and was influenced by them. Several people and several places could be named; but Charles Hamilton of Painshill occupies a special place, for the length of his association, for the variety of his points of contact, and, quite simply, for the firmness with which several of these contacts can be established.

In the course of these developments at Painshill and Stourhead, the contacts are in both directions, and are sometimes part of a more general activity, affecting other gardens around the same time. This is clearly the case with the earliest common feature, the wooden Palladian or 'Chinese' bridge – other versions being built at Virginia Water and at Kew in the same period. The strongly curved side view of these bridges not only led some visitors to think they were 'Chinese', but worried them that they might be unsafe. At Stourhead, Mrs Lybbe Powys had serious misgivings in 1776 – the bridge was 'pretty at a distance', but 'when near, the idea of going over a kind of ladder only is frightful. Another party of company could not bring themselves to venture, but 'tis not so bad after . . . a few steps' (Mrs Philip Lybbe Powys, *Passages from the Diaries of . . . 1756 to 1808*, ed. E.J.Climenson, 1899, pp.169–70).

After the Palladian bridges, there is no strong link between Painshill and Stourhead until 1762, when it is suddenly apparent that several garden visits have taken place. Henry Hoare's admiration for the temple of Bacchus at Painshill – 'all Attic Elegance' – is linked with two comparisons: 'It is an oblong, the Form of the Temple of Fortuna Virilis or the

[40]

Long Temple of Balbec'. Here we see his thoughts turning to Robert Wood's *Ruins of Balbec*, from which the inspiration for the temple of Apollo will be derived. At each stage, the buildings Henry Hoare puts up are usually grander, more solid than Hamilton's; he is aware of the possibility of comparison, and the element of imitation – and rivalry – is undoubtedly present.

In the later 1760s, Hamilton's influence grows stronger. His Turkish tent is directly imitated – one visitor saw it in 1766, and in September 1769 Sir John Parnell wrote in his journal that it was 'a Turkish tent taken from Mr. Hamilton's, very Elegant but rather inferior to his'. Parnell was the first to note the existence of the Gothic Convent, built in the 1760s, and situated in the woods north-west of Stourhead House. He referred to it as 'the Abbey in the wood', and this feature may have helped prompt Hamilton to build his 'ruined abbey' in 1772, and had even more influence on the young William Beckford, whose early thoughts for what was to become Fonthill Abbey included a 'convent in ruins'. Then, in 1771, the least classical, and most primitive of the features at Stourhead was built, the hermitage. Its construction with 'old Gouty nobbly oakes' referred to by Henry Hoare in a letter of 30 November 1771 is shown in the views by the Swedish artist F. M. Piper, made in 1779, and the interior must have been on a par with Hamilton's at Painshill. Hamilton had presumably been in contact with Henry Hoare again, since Hoare's letter mentions changes to the path leading up to the temple of Apollo, 'as Mr. Hamilton advised'. One of the oaks which might be used for the hermitage was so old that Henry Hoare was 'not quite sure it is not Anti Diluvian', an echo of the *pierre antidiluvienne* admired in Hamilton's grotto.

It is not known who designed or built the Stourhead hermitage. Flitcroft had died in 1769. If, as Henry Hoare wrote in his letter of 30 November 1771, Hamilton had 'advised' on a part of the scheme, could

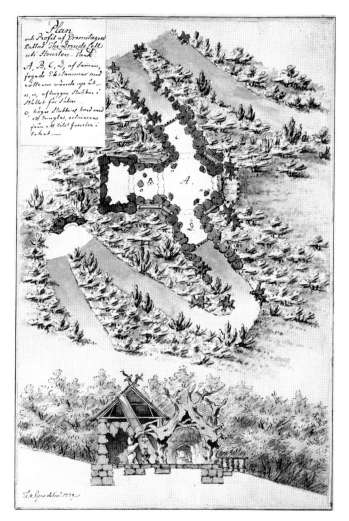

Plan and elevation of the Hermitage, called 'The Druid's Cell' (F. M. Piper, 1779).
Courtesy of the Kungl. Akademien för de Fria Konsterna, Stockholm

he have designed the whole? Another possibility is that Hamilton had recommended his grotto-maker Joseph Lane, who had just finished the enlargement of the grotto at Painshill. Lane, born at Tisbury near Fonthill in 1717, had recently been making grotto-constructions for Alderman Beckford (see ch. III below), and his presence in western Wiltshire would not have been improbable.

From the outside, the building was indeed grotto-like; yet inside, it was truly a hermitage in the Painshill style – John Wesley, at Stourhead in September 1776, writes of

> the castle-grotto, into which you enter unawares, beneath a heap of ruins. This is within totally built of roots of trees, wonderfully interwoven. On one side of it is a little hermitage, with a lamp, a chair, a table and bones upon it (*Journal*, VI, 128).

These details were no doubt inspired by talk with Hamilton. In his letter Henry Hoare adds the wry comment 'I believe I shall put it in to be myself The Hermit' (quoted in Woodbridge, *L.& A.*, p.62). Hamilton, as we know, is supposed to have hired a hermit - with a seven year contract, in which period the hermit was to have no contact with barber, beer or barmaid. One person was hired, 'but a three weeks' trial cured him' (John Timbs, *English Eccentrics and Eccentricities*, 1866, p.157). Such a ludicrous conclusion would not have been to Henry Hoare's taste at Stourhead, however important delight and enjoyment were in the nature of his gardens.

We may see a proper distinction between his attitude and that of other garden enthusiasts in Richard Graves' novel *Columella; or, the Distressed Anchoret* (2v., 1779). Here the hero – mainly modelled on William Shenstone, but with a touch of Henry Hoare's friend Bampfylde, who drew the two illustrations – is visited at his country home, and his garden is described. A miniature of Stourhead, it has a fine cascade, a ruined temple, a Roman bridge, a grotto and hermitage; but its enjoyment is soured – at times – by silly neighbours, by ignorant peasants, and by marauding pigs which have 'routed up' all Columella's newly-planted primroses and periwinkles. In contrast Stourhead itself is described in terms of the greatest respect (II, 5–13, 30–31).

Some days later the travellers visit Columella again, and find a matter of ridicule: a stranger has called, as 'he heard that the squire wanted an hermit'. Happily, Columella finds out in time that the 'hermit was a sad drunken dog', and had lost his last post – as a hermit – 'for getting the dairy-maid with child'. . . It is Hamilton's hermit-story over again.

We may contrast Bampfylde's comic image of Columella's garden with his superb vision of the view at Stourhead. The engraving was published in 1777, roughly contemporary with the frontispiece to *Columella* (1779). The view is taken from near the Pantheon, looking across the lake to the temple of Flora, the Roman bridge and the church. It is indeed 'a charming Gaspard picture'. Yet the foreground has hints, not of Gaspard, but of Watteau, painter of elegant *fêtes champêtres*, of 'garden parties' in Arcadian settings far removed from the cares of the world. A moment of delight – the instant of arrival from 'the little enchanting ocean', set within a cultured, meditated, gently poetic scene.

∗   ∗   ∗

Henry Hoare died in 1785. Already in 1783 he had retired to his house in London, making over his Stourhead estate to his grandson Richard Colt Hoare (1758–1838). Richard Colt Hoare appears to have maintained the Stourhead gardens with little change for some years – in 1785, after the death of his wife, in August, and the death of his grandfather in September, he went abroad, and apart from a short while in 1787, he was away from Stourhead (mainly in Italy) until 1791.

On his return in 1791, he settled into a scholarly career which lasted for the rest of his life. Articles and volumes on the history of Wiltshire followed from around 1800. His *History of Modern Wiltshire* (1822–44), vol.I (1822) and vol.V (1829) are important here for their long sections to do with the history of Stourhead and Fonthill. For Stourhead, we should note his comment on his grandfather's original and independent part in designing the gardens, and his own wish to 'render the design of

C. W. Bampfylde's frontispiece to *Columella*, by Richard Graves (1776).
A satirical view of the features of Stourhead

these gardens as chaste and correct as possible, and to give them the character of an Italian villa' (I, 66).

This wish might now seem puzzling, when the gardens have been managed with conspicuous care by the National Trust for several decades, and the plantings of trees and shrubs controlled, pruned or

View from the Chinese 'ombrello', showing the temple of Apollo, the Roman bridge
and the Pantheon (F. M. Piper, 1779). Courtesy of the Kungl. Akademien
för de Fria Konsterna, Stockholm

thinned with reference to their state towards the end of the 18th century.
But for Richard Colt Hoare, 'chaste and correct' was to do with the
buildings, a wish to return, architecturally, to the classical simplicity of
his grandfather's first scheme, with the Pantheon, the temple of Flora
and the grotto in a – relatively – open landscape. Certainly his own picture of the lake, with the Pantheon beyond, published in John Britton's
Beauties of Wiltshire (I, 1801, 17), suggests a simple alternation between
lawn and woodland which may surprise us today.

Richard Colt Hoare complained of 'nature overcrowded with buildings', and so many of them were removed. By 1792, the Turkish tent
had gone; by 1798, the wooden, curved Palladian bridge; by 1814, the
hermitage, leaving only a stony alcove beside the path. Other buildings,
including an open temple, the 'greenhouse of false Gothic' seen by

Walpole, the Chinese alcove, the Chinese 'ombrello', and the very English revolving tub all disappeared in these years.

From about 1791 onwards Richard Colt Hoare also began to vary and enrich the shrubs and trees. In his grandfather's time, beech, oak, sycamore, yew and fir had provided most of the plantation – with the simple idea expressed by Henry Hoare around 1752 that

> the greens should be ranged together in large masses as the shades are in paintings: to contrast the dark masses with light ones, and to relieve each dark mass itself with little sprinklings of lighter greens here and there (in Spence, *Observations*, item 1105).

This attitude, common in the mid-18th century, and more to do with painting than with plants, was rejected by Richard Colt Hoare, who intoduced many new species to the gardens, including Rhododendron ponticum in 1791. His plantings of ornamental species were followed by further introductions, in the mid- and later 19th century, and again in the first half of the 20th century, substantially affecting the density of the shrub and woodland coverage, and the seasonal colouring (details are given in K. Woodbridge, 'The Planting of Ornamental Shrubs at Stourhead', in *Garden History*, IV, 1 (Spring 1976), 88–109).

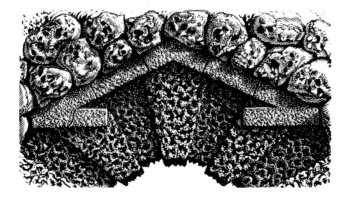

III

'Magna Charta in his Hand'

Alderman William Beckford acquired the four to five thousand acres of the Fonthill estate in the early 1740s, shortly before becoming M.P. for Shaftesbury (1747–54). There was already a substantial house at Fonthill, built in the mid-17th century for Sir Francis Cottington. We do not know in what condition Beckford found the property, nor what use he made of it at first. His private, business and political life in London was hectic, and would seem to have kept him there most of the time. His town house was in Soho Square (now no. 22), and it was there that his son, William Thomas Beckford, was born at the end of September 1760, and that he himself died ten years later, on 21 June 1770.

The Alderman was a man of immense vitality, matched by his wealth (derived from sugar plantations in Jamaica). Crude and direct in his ways, he had energy – and courage – to stand up for political ideals, as he did in addressing the famous 'Remonstrance' to George III in May 1770. This energy shows equally in his private life. He did not marry until 1756, but had by then sired a number of bastards. His one legitimate son, William Beckford, remarked to Cyrus Redding in the 1830s 'My father had scores of natural children' (Redding, *Memoirs of William Beckford of Fonthill*, 2v., 1859, II, 299), and Walpole modifies this only slightly in his reference to the fire which consumed Fonthill in February 1755. Then, wrote Walpole, Beckford remarked with phlegm 'Oh! I have an odd fifty thousand pounds in a drawer. I will build it up again: it won't be above a thousand pounds apiece difference to my thirty children' (to R. Bentley, 23 Feb. 1755, in Walpole, *Correspondence*, XXXV, 211).

'Well, we must build it up again' – this was the more simple, and discreet, phrase in Redding's biography (I, 275). In all this, one should note the difference between Beckford's wealth, and Charles Hamilton's modest means at Painshill.

Beckford's new house was virtually complete by 1769. It was large, costly, and quickly called – by others, if not by the Alderman – Fonthill Splendens. A huge Palladian mansion, its basic plan resembled that of Colen Campbell's Houghton Hall in Norfolk – a central pile, with matching service wings, one to each side, connected by passages and curving colonnades. Plans and elevations appear in the 1769 volume of *Vitruvius Britannicus* by John Woolfe and James Gandon.

Set beside Colen Campbell's smaller Palladian design at Stourhead, the scale of Alderman Beckford's new house is ostentatious. In September 1769 Sir John Parnell said of it 'the House is one of the most magnificent in England, a noble colonnade connecting two offices [i.e. service wings] of I believe 60 feet square to a house about 140 by 80, all roofed with copper . . . There are about 25 rooms furnished with the utmost expense, gilding etc . . . .'.

Parnell clearly thought that the statues were lacking in taste – notably one of Beckford himself, 'in marble dressed as Mayor of London, Magna charta in his hand and the true stiff tye wigg on, which one may conceive makes a pretty classical figure in Parian marble' (this work, by J.F. Moore, and dated 1763, now belongs to the Ironmongers' Company of London).

* * *

We do not know when Alderman Beckford started the improvement of gardens and park at Fonthill, nor even whether some part of the work

'Fonthill, splendens, Anno 1805' (John Buckler, in Sir Richard Colt Hoare,
History of Modern Wiltshire, 1829)

had been begun by the Cottingtons before him. What there is on
Alderman Beckford's garden-making is slight. There are however two
accounts by visitors, one by Pococke in 1754, the other by Parnell in
1769, which occur at crucial moments in the history of Fonthill. The
first is just a few months before the 1755 fire, which destroyed the house
Beckford had bought, and the second comes shortly before the Alderman's death – which suspended garden development at Fonthill for over
ten years. A few pictures help to confirm or clarify what they wrote, as
do a few later accounts written before the Alderman's son William
Beckford had changed much of the earlier scheme.

The area which was developed lay mainly along the course of the
Fonthill stream, which runs from north to south (from Fonthill Bishop
towards Tisbury) in a slight valley, some two or three hundred yards

from the site of Fonthill Splendens. The ground rises on the western and southern sides of the house, and also on the eastern side of the stream. Whether this stream had already been dammed to form fish-ponds (as had been the case at Stourhead) before Beckford bought the estate, we do not know, but the surviving views of the original house (built for the Mervyns in the later 16th century) and its enlarged successor built for the Cottingtons after 1631 show neither stream or lake of any size.

By 1753–54 much had changed. In his garden and landscape developments Alderman Beckford had to begin from scratch – not quite so much as Hamilton at Painshill, but still with little done before his time. In Richard Colt Hoare's *History of Modern Wiltshire*, I, plates II–IV, the earliest house is named 'Fonthill Antiquus', to show the difference of the next house (the Cottington's), named 'Fonthill Redivivus'. Beside these pictures, Pococke's account of 1754 (*Travels*, II, 44) gives us evidence of many new things.

First, there is the lake – known since as Fonthill Lake – made from a mile-and-a-half length of the Fonthill stream, running north to south, and some way eastwards from the Alderman's house. This lake – in Pococke's words 'a broad serpentine river' – formed by means of a dam at the lower end, is in exactly the manner of the 'landscape lakes' which Lancelot 'Capability' Brown had been making in England since the 1740s. Though in imitation of Brown's style, it is no puny echo, but a full-scale achievement, admirable today, and one of the principal parts of the Fonthill landscape to survive. It is not known who designed it – any more than most of the scores of similar 'landscape lakes' created in England in imitation of Brown's style from the mid-18th century onwards. Over the lake the Alderman had ordered a sturdy bridge – Pococke called it 'a very handsom bridge of free stone . . . of three arches, with a stone baluster'. Southwards, 'beyond the park, and op-

Fonthill – the Entrance Gateway (T. Higham, in John Rutter,
Delineations of Fonthill, 1823)

posite to the grand front [of the house] Mr. Beckford has built a
Church, on the plan of Covent garden, which is a good termination of
the prospect. There is a large lawn that way . . .'. Pococke goes on to
mention 'plantations' on the rising ground to the west, and so far his
account tallies with the engravings. Slight discrepancy comes with the
buildings in, or beside, the 'plantations' – one engraving shows a small
classical façade peeping through the lower edge of the trees, and the top
sections of a pagoda, no less, on the skyline, while Pococke, writing a
little later, says that there is 'an open temple on the side of the hill, and
an open rotundo is building higher up on the hill'. Presumably the
Alderman had changed his mind – unlike Charles Hamilton, he could
afford to do so.

Pococke mentions one other feature in another part of the grounds –
'to the north is a grand gateway near the village' (Fonthill Bishop). This
gateway – it is very grand – was first attributed to Inigo Jones, but

[53]

recent historians have preferred the 18th-century architect John Vardy, suggesting that he based his design on one by Jones.

Then came the fire. In the *Gentleman's Magazine* for February 1755 it read 'Wednesday 12. A sudden fire broke out at the seat of Wm Beckford, Esq., at Fonthill . . . which in three hours time consumed the greatest part of the building'. That building had contained 'many modern paintings all over it as well as on the ceilings, and a handsom library'. All the contents of the house were burnt, and the Alderman not only rebuilt the vast mansion others were to call 'Fonthill Splendens', but collected and commissioned more paintings and sculptures. By 1756 his new house was far enough built for him to live there, and to bring with him his wife, Maria Marsh (née Hamilton, the niece of Charles Hamilton of Painshill), married the same year. The only child of their marriage, William Thomas Beckford, was born in 1760.

John Parnell's scorn for the Alderman's house and its contents was considerable. His views, in 1769, on the gardens and park are no less scathing. Only one building is mentioned – the bridge. This is

> an hideous piece of architecture scarcely fitt for the most private part of a trading City only tolerable as being strong enough to bear perpetual waggons. I never saw such a thing in my life in the Regions of taste built as an ornament.

De gustibus. Pococke had called it a 'very handsom bridge', and William Gilpin called it it 'a very sumptuous bridge. If the bridge had been more simple, the scene about it would have been more pleasing' (*Observations on the Western Parts of England*, written late 1770s, published 1798). Parnell for his part goes on to attack the planting:

> A knoll covered with well grown old trees on one side and a piece of water on the other leaves scarce place for so great a Pile as the

House and offices to stand in and the Paltry little Evergreen
clumps Particularly scots firr crowding on the Brow of the knoll
and under the old Sycamores Oak &c. on it add to the smallness of
the Lawn and makes the House preposterous . . .

Some later writers (J. C. Loudon in 1835, Lansdown in 1844) contrast
the general bareness of the surrounding Wiltshire downland with the
densely wooded estate at Fonthill, planted mainly by the Alderman's
son. It may be that the Alderman had already begun such plantings, or
that the changes related to the building of Splendens in 1755 and
onwards had entailed further landscaping. Parnell does not mention the
garden buildings – temple and rotunda (or pagoda) – seen in 1753–54. If
they had already gone, their removal may have been part of a new planting scheme.

Certainly the house stood in full view of the public road, and its huge
size may have made it seem out of scale. No doubt to the younger
William Beckford, its lack of privacy (which would never have given his
ebullient father a moment's concern) was a reason for building Fonthill
Abbey so much further within the estate.

*   *   *

There are several features from the Alderman's time which deserve
notice. On the eastern side of the lake, there was the quarry, which was
opened up to provide stone for the building of Splendens in 1755
onwards. It was a handy source, and the bridge over the lake – 'handsom' or 'hideous' as it may have been – would have been admirably sited.
The quarry however left unsightly gashes in the hillside – 'some of the
white cavities . . . yawned full in front of the house in a manner offensive
to all persons of taste' (Britton, *op. cit.*, I, 241–2) – and so the Alderman
had it 'thickly planted with firs of different kinds' (Redding, *op. cit.*, II,

80). The quarry site later became the Alpine garden – with a grotto by Josiah Lane (son of Joseph Lane) developed by his son William Beckford in the mid-1790s (see ch. IV below).

Near the northern tip of the lake, on its western side (only 150 yards away from Vardy's gateway on the public road) is the boathouse, which served also as a cold bath. It is not mentioned until 1791, in the travel journal of the Dutchman, Baron J. F. W. van Spaen van Biljoen, where it is called a 'grotto' – 'a particularly fine one with a cold bath' (see H. Tromp, 'A Dutchman's Visits to some English Gardens in 1791', *Journal of Garden History*, II, 1 (1982), 49), and it appears in one of J. M.W. Turner's Fonthill views of 1799 (now held by the City Art Galleries, Leeds). In 1823, Rutter attributes it to the Alderman's period, and its use of rustication is stylistically similar to that of the gateway. It might therefore be by the same architect, Vardy.

Now recently and rather insensitively restored, it remains a remarkable building – 'like a crypt of nave and aisles, only of course flooded' (N. Pevsner, *Wiltshire*, 1975, p.249). Originally with a three-arched open-

Fonthill – the Boat House
(in John Rutter, *Delineations of Fonthill*, 1823)

ing onto the lake, it contains a long, covered dock, with a circular 'pool' – or bathing-place – at the inner end, enclosed to the sides and rear by a paved jetty. It was here most probably that the younger William Beckford 'bathed in the river every day until some time in November' (B. Alexander, *Life at Fonthill*, 1957, p.25).

Still on the western shore of the lake, some hundreds of yards south of the boathouse, is the hermitage, or hermit's cave. On rising ground overlooking the lake, it is hidden from the road behind a stand of trees, and the entrance – framed with giant flints – is suitably shaded and enclosed. It is a sizeable cavern cut in the chalk, with a roughly-vaulted roof and the remains of a seated, draped figure set in one wall. The shape of the hermitage is not far different from that of the main grotto-chamber at Painshill, by Joseph Lane. Above ground, a few yards distant, is what Rutter termed in 1823 'a rude erection in imitation of a cromlech'. It is a memorable object made from rough slabs of rock piled into crooked columns, forming a small roofless 'staircase' rising up ten or twelve feet, and smothered, even possibly supported, by knotty, twining stems of ivy. This structure is so crude, so primitive in its appearance that it barely looks like 'architecture' – and in this, it has again a close affinity to the knobbly spikes and part-arch, part-cave-wall which Joseph Lane piled up among the dark laurels, yews and cedars close to the grotto at Painshill.

Close to the entrance to the hermitage is a tunnel, rough and dark, which leads under the public road to the grounds south of the site of Splendens. Though this tunnel might have been made at the same time as the hermitage and the cromlech, I prefer to think that it came later, made for the Alderman's son, as part of his schemes to achieve greater privacy.

Last of these features added by the Alderman, but never completed, was a tower. On Stop or Stop's Beacon (now marked 'Beacon Hill' on the

O.S. maps, and 777' above sea level), one and a half miles south-west of Splendens, Beckford began to erect 'a magnificent tower . . . of triangular form, having a circular bastion at each of its angles' (J. Storer, *A Description of Fonthill Abbey*, 1812, quoted in L. Melville, *op. cit.*, p. 356). This, as Rutter pointed out, was begun in imitation of Alfred's Tower at Stourhead. The triangular tower for Stourhead had been proposed by Henry Hoare as early as 1762, and Henry Flitcroft had supplied the design. Progress had been slow, but in 1769–70 the project had begun to accelerate (it was completed in 1772), and Beckford's idea may well have been to 'do better' than his neighbour. But with the Alderman's death in 1770 work seems to have stopped. Many years later, in 1812, Storer wrote that 'the foundations are entirely laid, and in most parts the walls are raised to the height of nine or ten feet'.

Today the outline still remains, the low foundations of the wall (some two to four feet high) extending in a vast equilateral triangle over the summit of the hill. In the summer of 1990, my friends and I pushed through head-high bracken and fallen pine branches to arrive at a rough measure of 75' along each side, with a further 15' at each end, being the distance across the 'circular bastion' at each corner of the triangle – making roughly 100' from one corner to another (see 'Twin Towers', by C. Thacker, Steven Ashley and Julian Berry, *Georgian Group Journal*, 1995, pp. 115–8).

Stop's Beacon is a little-visited spot, the highest on the Fonthill estate, now dark with conifers. Had the Alderman lived to build this tower to a height appropriate to its horizontal extent, it would have soared above Hoare's triangular building (likewise in a far-off part of the Stourhead woods), just as Hoare's tower was built bigger – and stranger – than Hamilton's four-sided Gothic tower or belvedere in the remote western corner of Painshill. We might note that Alfred's Tower at Stourhead was intended from the start as a patriotic monument, and

Alderman William Beckford (1707–1770)

that Alderman Beckford at Fonthill saw himself firmly in the guise of the patriot citizen, standing up for the rights of Englishmen against oppression in whatever form. Was this last monument not only 'doing better' than Henry Hoare in architectural terms (as Splendens had out-done the mansion at Stourhead), but in terms of patriotism as well?

It is right to add that there are two further stages in this tower-sequence, since the younger William Beckford also thought to build a tower (four-sided, in the Gothic style, and 175 feet tall) on Stop or Stop's Beacon. This was the earliest form of his idea for a retreat far away from his father's Palladian glories at Splendens. The idea was then several times modified, and the final site was on Hinkley Hill, not Stop's Beacon – while the building itself, the Abbey, had the tallest tower of them all.

As with most of the garden structures at Splendens, we do not know which architect the Alderman had chosen for his proposed tower. Flitcroft, who designed Alfred's Tower for Henry Hoare, had died in 1769, and there is no record of his ever being employed by the Alderman. Could it have been Charles Hamilton, or someone brought in on Hamilton's advice? By 1769–70, Hamilton had visited Fonthill several times (once, in 1766, in conjunction with a visit to Stourhead. See N. Kitz, *op. cit.*, p. 87). His grotto-builder in the 1760s, Joseph Lane, apparently worked at Fonthill in the same decade, making the hermitage and the 'cromlech' nearby.

*   *   *

Of the Alderman's creation, only Fonthill lake and a handful of features remain – the quarry, since overgrown with trees and bushes, and pierced here and there with the younger William Beckford's labyrinth of grotto-caves; the great gateway across the public road, enlarged with lodges and pompous flanking walls in the mid-19th century; the boathouse, collapsing and now partly sunk into the waters of the lake; Joseph Lane's hermitage and nearby 'cromlech'; and the low foundations of a tower, which was never more than a few feet high. All the rest has gone – the church, the temples, or temple and pagoda; and Splendens itself, all gone – mostly dismantled to make young William Beckford's even greater mansion, the gigantic edifice of Fonthill Abbey. Yet the Alderman's lake, his enormous house, his garden features, whether they survive or not today, were all the setting – and indeed the framework – for William Beckford's heroic garden, woodland, lake and abbey creation in the decades following his father's death. Fonthill Splendens is where William Beckford grew up, and lived, most of the time until his early twenties; and where, when he was in England, he lived until 1807. Not until he was 47 years old did he leave Splendens, to move into his own building, the Abbey.

Yet even then, though the vulgarity of Splendens was put aside, his pride in his father's strength of character was maintained. At Splendens the statue of the Alderman, with his 'true stiff tye wigg on', had remained in a prominent position in the largest of the public rooms – the ballroom or 'great gallery'. In 1807 it was taken to the Abbey and again given a principal setting, in the great hall; and in 1822 William Beckford took the statue with him to Bath, where it received similar honours – the statue of the Lord Mayor of London, 'Magna charta in his hand'.

IV

'We may Seek the Green Solitudes'

When Alderman Beckford died in 1770, his son William Beckford was nine. Most of his life had been spent at Fonthill in his father's great mansion. For a decade therefore he had lived amid the bustle of entertainment, among a flow of visitors – his father's political friends, his mother's relatives, and neighbours from nearby estates, such as Henry Hoare and the group from Stourhead, who, in the summer of 1754, 'took a gallop over the Downs . . . with Mr. Barton cum multis aliis to Mr. Beckford' (in Woodbridge, *L.& A.*, p.571).

His father's death reduced social activity at Splendens, but it did not stop. Young Beckford's preferences for companions may not have been what his mother thought best, while he often considered the adult company at Fonthill dull or philistine. He was a brilliant child, and must quickly have seen that he was far cleverer than many of those around him. It cannot have been long before he knew also that he was to be master of an exceptional fortune.

From the mid-60s until his coming of age in 1781 his education was entrusted to a series of tutors (his mother, a Methodist, and fearful that he would be exposed to unsuitable influences, never let him go to school or university), notably Robert Drysdale from 1768, and then the Rev John Lettice from 1771 or '72. The Rev Samuel Henley was partly mentor, partly friend, in the early eighties. Apart from a brief experience of instruction from the youthful Mozart, Beckford is said to have had lessons in architecture from Sir William Chambers, and, most important, lessons in drawing from Alexander Cozens (c.1717–86), a drawing-master at Eton from 1763 till the mid-70s.

Beckford learnt French almost as early as he did English, and Latin soon followed, then Italian, Portuguese and Spanish. His interests and reading showed a marked preference for what we might call exotic, romantic or 'sublime' themes. Much has been written about his continued enthusiasm for Oriental tales and images, fed from the *Arabian Nights* and the welter of real or pretended translations from eastern literature which appeared in French or English in the 18th century. In 1773, Lettice made him burn a cherished collection of Oriental drawings (most likely supplied by Cozens) which were thought to be unsuitable.

But this did not stop Beckford's passion for things Oriental, and Cozens' influence continued. Writing in 1775 to his friend George Douglas, Earl of Morton, then at Eton, Beckford refers to Cozens as 'the Persian', and makes eager suggestions for the plot and décor of a puppet play which Morton was proposing to produce. Beckford's ideas include the final scene, which is the first reference to his interest in gardens: 'It should represent a delightful garden. The sixth scene composed of trees bending under a profusion of fruit and flowers; at the end a large rock partly bare, partly covered with bushy wood, a cascade streaming down its peak. Above, a clear tranquil sky with domes obelisks and other gay edifices just peeping over the tips of the shrubs' (in Alexander, *op. cit.*, p.44, and Kim Sloan, *Alexander & John Robert Cozens*, 1986, p.74). This passage is written over a sketch, presumably by Beckford, of a wild, rocky landscape, with a cave, and bushes, and a sarcophagus. His garden interest begins as it will continue...

*   *   *

Beckford's mother (the 'Begum' as he called her) sent him with his tutor Lettice to Switzerland from autumn 1777 to November 1778, to live with Hamilton relatives near Geneva. There he flourished, meeting new and stimulating people, and recording his experience in long letters – particularly to Alexander Cozens, and to his half-sister Elizabeth Marsh (later Mrs Hervey). He met the aged Voltaire (who died a year later), and met and became intimate with the Huber family (Jean Huber, artist and writer, was a friend of Voltaire's at Ferney). His reading extended, adding to things Eastern the poems of Gray and Ossian, the tragic and melancholy *Sorrows of Werther*, Scandinavian mythology, the chivalric fantasy of Ariosto, and violent episodes from the *Inferno*, such as the tale of Ugolino. To these, all confirmed in his correspondence, I would add the certain influence of Rousseau's *Nouvelle Héloïse* and *Émile*.

At this early moment in Beckford's career, we must note his overridingly emotional appreciation of landscape, which he sees as a consoling alternative to the dullness of society.

After writing to Elizabeth Hervey of the constraint, the mediocrity, the lack of imagination involved in living as the average English gentleman did when travelling abroad, he exclaims 'Were I not to hear from you sometimes, to see a Genius or two sometimes, to go to Voltaire's sometimes and to the Mountains very often, I should die' (3 October 1777, in Oliver, *op. cit.*, p. 22).

'To the Mountains very often'. Many of Beckford's letters from Switzerland are to do with landscape and gardens, and anticipate his later creation at Fonthill. It often remains, I admit, vague and fantastical – like his incomplete, spasmodic fiction, written in 1777, and named *The Vision* by Guy Chapman when it was first published in 1930. Here are mountain vistas, grottoes, subterranean volcanoes and tempests. While much is in an oriental vein, foreshadowing the unique and concentrated exotisme of his *Vathek*, written in 1782, the fascination with wild and lonely landscape is equally strong, and will remain as a central part of Beckford's way of thinking (or feeling). Read the opening lines:

I happened accidentally to open my Casement: the Moon shone
bright in the clear sky illuminating the Mountains. I stole away
silently from the gay circle of Company and passing swiftly the
Garden of Flowers, the Orange trees and the Grove betwixt the
House and the Rocks set my feet to some steps cut in their solid
sides . . . (*The Vision*, p. 3).

To the end of his life, Beckford was to behave in this way (or to wish
that he could). In letters and travel journals, he will tell how he 'stole
away . . . from the gay circle of Company', and how he would forsake the
formal gardens round his father's or his host's mansion to wander on his
own in the wilder countryside beyond. In *The Vision*, his solitary mountain wanderings are punctuated by moments when he reclines on the
ground, gazing dreamily at the landscape: 'I lay a few moments on the
bank' (p. 9) . . . 'I sunk down on the grass' (p. 12) . . . 'I would lay me down
on the soft herbage by the brink of a bubbling spring and muse . . . Thus
passed I know not how many hours steeped in delights' (p. 72).

The image of the young, and wealthy, Beckford reclining on a grassy
bank to dream may be matched appropriately with the painting by
Joseph Wright of Derby of Sir Brooke Boothby, painted in 1781, and
now in the Tate Gallery. Here Boothby lies by a woodland stream, in
casual but elegant clothes, and holding a negligently folded manuscript
written by his hero, the persecuted and nature-loving Rousseau. *The
Vision* was addressed to Alexander Cozens, and in a letter to Cozens at
the time Beckford makes clear the kind of 'nature' which he associates
with a garden, and the uses he conceives for it:

Reserve with care your System of sentimental Gardening, the time
may come perhaps when we shall execute it. Yes, that time may
arrive when we may seek the green solitudes and roam about
Foreign Mountains, when we may sit together in such a Valley as I

Sir Brooke Boothby (Joseph Wright of Derby, 1781).
Courtesy of the Tate Gallery

have described and gaze at the last gleams of departing Day. How should I delight to wander with you thro' remote forests and pitch our Tents by Moonlight in a Wilderness . . . (24 November 1777, in Melville, *op. cit.*, p. 37).

'Your System of sentimental Gardening' – there is no further word of this in Beckford's letters, nor any mention of it among the many 'systems' elaborated by Alexander Cozens.

From Geneva he made several excursions on his own to Mont Salève. Then, in June 1778, he travelled with Lettice to visit the Carthusian monastery of the Grande Chartreuse. At both places he indulged in long day-dreams, letting his thoughts drift in harmony with the imagined mood of the landscape. While his ardent reactions to mountainous solitude may have been influenced by the letters of Thomas Gray (who had visited the monastery with Horace Walpole in 1739), they were also encouraged by personal pride. Among Beckford's properties was a 2300-acre estate at Witham, in Somerset, the site of the first Carthusian monastery in England. The monks had learnt this fact, and were accordingly respectful towards him. In Beckford's time the real Witham no longer held any spectacular ruins, and was not in any physical way the inspiration of Fonthill Abbey. Yet the idea of this earliest Carthusian foundation in England was strong, and may have formed part of Beckford's wish to build a 'ruined convent' in a remote, elevated spot such as Stop's Beacon at Fonthill.

Beckford and Lettice stayed at the monastery for three days, and Beckford's extended, emotional account (in his *Dreams, Waking Thoughts and Incidents* [1783], published with the *History of the Caliph Vathek* in 1891, pp.270–293) shows him to have been in a state of continuous imaginative exaltation. Several times, by day and by night, he wandered off into the sombre, pine-clad mountains, pondering the life of St. Bruno, founder of the Order, and the desirability of an existence far from the world, given over to solitary meditation – and all within the sublimest natural surroundings of forest, hanging rocks, precipices, torrents, storms, sunset, moonlight or dawn. Much of this recurs in his long and passionately developed creation of Fonthill Abbey, both in the building and the surrounding domain. His initial ideas included both a solitary tower, and a 'ruined convent', set high on a remote and pine-girt hilltop. Though the idea was to change, and change again, much of the sublimity of this first conception was to be achieved, not least the seclusion of the building, and the solitary life Beckford was to lead within its walls, and within the vast walled garden-forest-wilderness he created round the Abbey.

*   *   *

Though scathingly contemptuous of those whom he thought dull or pretentious, Beckford was by no means unsocial during his year in Switzerland. He was not averse to garden parties. Descriptions of three such occasions, held at the same spot on the shore of Lake Geneva, but spaced over some fifteen years (in 1777, 1783 and 1792), show vividly the character of these events, and the changing relationship of Beckford with those around him, and with society as a whole.

The first party was given by his host and relative Colonel Hamilton in August 1777, and described by Beckford, writing to his aunt, Lady Effingham (quoted in Alexander, *op. cit.*, pp.61–2). The scene was by the lake shore, backed by the woods of Blonay, a few miles east of Evian. 'An irregular lawn, surrounded by firs, sloped gradually down to the Lake; a cleft in the jagged rocks gave a distant view of blue peaks, and an invisible cataract thundered down the mountain.' In this 'natural' setting, the many guests paraded, enjoyed a cold collation, and – in elegant dresses and bemedalled uniforms – danced to music from an orchestra partly hidden among the trees. The music and the dancing continued long after nightfall, until rowing boats arrived to carry the guests back to Evian. As the moonlight shone over the lake, the voices of singers rose into the summer night. 'It may be the happiest day of my life, such another may never return' said Beckford to one of his partners.

Return it did, six years later. On August 10 1783, Beckford himself held a similar party at the same spot. In May 1783, he had married Lady Margaret Gordon, and their honeymoon took them to Switzerland. This time the party was wholly in the long summer evening, illuminated 'by enormous tapers', fastened high up in the chestnut trees. Mirrors helped, as did the 'interesting glow of sunset' – resembling the 'Gardens of the Hesperides' (quoted in Alexander, *op. cit.*, p.107).

By the time of the third party, in 1792, Beckford could no longer term himself a happy man. In March 1784, he and his wife had returned to

England, and in the autumn of 1784, while they were guests at Powderham Castle in Devon, the homosexual relationship between Beckford and young William Courtenay provoked public scandal. What happened between them is not clear. But the public reaction was decisive. Beckford's political and social career in England was at an end. A peerage, which he had hoped to receive at the end of 1784, was withdrawn. While Lady Margaret, his wife, stayed with him loyally (she died in Switzerland two years later, in May 1786), his neighbours closed their doors to him. Ostracised, he stayed away from England for most of the next fifteen years, embittered with English society, and rebuffed in his attempts to be hospitable. From 1785 onwards, most of his closer acquaintances were to be foreigners, whom he met on his restless travels abroad. In this context, a singular episode in the summer of 1792 completes this sequence of three garden parties. Beckford was again by the shore of Lake Geneva, living outside Evian, when he briefly made the acquaintance of 'Buck' Whaley, a rich and eccentric young Irishman. Whaley had been staying in Lausanne, on the north side of Lake Geneva. Foreign friends, all aristocrats, proposed an excursion across the lake to visit Beckford, and they, with Whaley, spent many hours in Beckford's company. After meeting him in Evian round midday, they moved near to Blonay. Whaley's description echoes the earlier scenes of 1777 and 1783:

> The carriages were summoned: the whole company was conveyed in coaches-and-four, and on about twenty saddle horses, to the distance of about four miles, where we arrived at a most delightful wood, in the midst of which was a garden laid out in the English taste, adorned with statues, and here and there with clumps of the most odoriferous flowering shrubs. Here, while we sauntered, our ears were often unexpectedly struck with the softest music, the

performers of which were to us invisible, and the sounds were reverberated, with ravishing melody, by the echoing mountains which surrounded us so that the whole appeared the effect of enchantment (Buck Whaley, *Memoirs*, ed. Sir E. Sullivan, 1906, pp. 295–296).

After a ball continuing to the next morning, Whaley and his friends went back over the lake to Lausanne, and the following day he met the aged historian, Edward Gibbon. The visit to Beckford was described, and Gibbon showed his full disapproval: 'It was astonishing any Englishman would visit a man who lay under such an imputation as Mr. B— ... and he [Gibbon] would venture to say, that I [Whaley] was the only one among my countrymen who had ever paid that man the smallest attention since his banishment' (ibid., p. 298).

*　　*　　*

Beckford was however to travel, to experience, to suffer, and to do a great deal more, including gardening, before this last garden party near Blonay in 1792, and some account should be taken of his earlier life, travels and related writings, since they lead conclusively to his creation at Fonthill.

Returned from his first visit to Switzerland at the end of 1778, Beckford was sent off, with Lettice, on an English tour in the summer of 1779. He went west, as far as Plymouth and Mount Edgcumbe, and then up to Bath, and beyond; visiting his elderly relative Charles Hamilton, who had left Painshill for Bath in 1773, living – and gardening – at 14 Royal Crescent.

The next year he set off – again with Lettice – on a 'Grand Tour' which lasted from June 1780 until April 1781. The goal was Naples, via Holland, Germany, the Alps, and northern and central Italy. In Holland

and Germany, he poured out scorn on formal gardens:

> Utrecht, July 2nd. . . endless avenues, and stiff parterres scrawled
> and flourished in patterns, like the embroidery of an old maid's
> work-bag'; and in Germany, at Schwetzingen, where he admired
> much of the leafy and well-planted scheme, he was cross when the
> gardener 'dragged [him] away to a sunburnt, contemptible
> hillock, commanding the view of a serpentine ditch, and decorated
> with the title of Jardin Anglois (in *Dreams, Waking Thoughts and
> Incidents*, pp. 113–114, 131).

Such formal or feeble scenes were far outweighed by natural beauty
and grandeur, and he indulged to the full his love of solitary wandering.
Near Mainz, he writes,

> hiring a skiff, I rowed about a mile down the stream, and landed on
> a sloping meadow, level with the waters, and newly-mown. Heaps
> of hay still lay dispersed under the copses which hemmed in on
> every side this little sequestered paradise. What a spot for a tent! I
> could encamp here for months, and never be tired. Not a day would
> pass without discovering some new promontory, some untrodden
> pasture, some unsuspected vale, where I might remain among
> woods and precipices lost and forgotten (ibid., p.126).

Near Ulm, they view the Danube, and the grassy, level shores remind
him of an account he has read of

> such vast and flowery meads in the interior of America, to which
> the roving tribes of Indians repair once or twice in a century . . .
> the highest ideas they entertain of future felicity consist in the per-
> petual enjoyment of songs and dances upon the green boundless
> lawns of their elysium (ibid., p.132).

His travel account is filled with such interludes. There follow day-dreams in villas, and in the gardens of the Carthusians at Venice and along the Brenta, alternating with musical delights, or visits to palaces, churches and ancient monuments. Gloom of mountains, in the Apennines, then the Boboli gardens in Florence, seen in twilight, and then, near Lucca, the garden of the villa Garzoni, where he drowses beside the statue of the goddess of Fame . . .

By November 1780 he had reached Naples, where he stayed for most of a month with Sir William and Lady Hamilton. They entertained him generously, for he was a relative. Sir William was frequently occupied with court and diplomatic business, and so Beckford saw a great deal of Lady Hamilton, whom he deeply admired, not only for musical talent, but for her character. He confided freely in her, so that she was quickly aware of his dreamy, introspective nature, and his sexual inclinations.

Not that her repeated urgings to him, to shun the 'enervating', 'pestilential' air of Italy, involving 'fatal corruption' and 'eternal infamy' (see Oliver, *op. cit.*, pp. 49–65) had much effect. His preference for private, imaginative freedom could not be quelled. On his way back to England, he wrote to her from Paris about his passion for music, which he agreed was separating him from those solemn people who held dullness to be a necessary part of respectability. Unrepentant, Beckford added

> I fear I shall never be half so sapient, nor good for anything in this world, but composing airs, building towers, forming gardens, collecting old Japan, and writing a journey to China or the moon (2 April 1781, in Oliver, *op. cit.*, p. 65).

This was a singularly accurate prediction. At the centre were two activities, *building towers*, and *forming gardens*, which stayed with him for the rest of his life. Back in England, he found himself the focus of his own coming of age celebrations. Not only had the festivities to be planned and organised, but lists of invitations had to be drawn up, and letters sent out; and behind all this, reponsibilities loomed – Parliament, public life, and marriage. Beckford's celebrations took place on 29 and 30 September 1781. On the 29th, apart from 300 guests at Splendens, between ten and twelve thousand local inhabitants had arrived for free beer and some food . . . Music, fireworks and bonfires followed at night. Next day, Sunday, Lettice gave the sermon in church, and there was another concert that night. By Monday, all but the intimes had gone. Beckford himself was free (and of age), and at liberty to plan his own, private celebrations for Christmas that year. The party was to include only those whom he wanted – a dozen or so, mostly round his own age – with his chosen singers and musicians to entertain them. Wholly within the walls of Splendens, with oriental décor and lighting by de Loutherbourg, it lasted three days and nights. The party's exotic extravagance, and its exclusivity, stimulated the envy of others, and their malice. No doubt, the extended nocturnal scenes were a powerful inspiration for the subterranean, infernal 'Halls of Eblis', in his *Vathek*, written the next year.

After a hectic social season in London (he participated with Lady Craven in the production of an operetta, she writing most of the libretto, he most of the music), he set off again for Naples. This time, he went as an adult, himself in charge of a princely suite – so grand that in Italy he was more than once thought to be the Emperor of Austria, travelling incognito. His companion-attendants were the musician John Burton, his physician Dr Ehrhart, Lettice the tutor, and the brilliant water-colourist John Robert Cozens, son of Alexander Cozens. In this way Beckford was able both to protect himself against unpleasantness, and to surround himself with persons who might give him appropriate aesthetic, cultural or emotional support. It is oddly like the arrangements made by the Prince in Goethe's *Triumph der Empfindsamkeit* (written

Lake Albano and Castel Gandolfo (John Robert Cozens, 1782).
Courtesy of the Victoria and Albert Museum

1778, published 1787), who was so sensitive, that he could not bear the crude incongruities of the real world, and so, when travelling, took with him a Naturmeister, or Directeur de la nature, who created portable scenery – *eine Reisenatur* – to represent forests, grottoes and arbours, which could be erected round the Prince when he stopped on his journeys. In Beckford's case, and with immense significance for Fonthill, the presence of John Robert Cozens cannot be underestimated. Cozens had already travelled on the Continent, and Beckford had admired his work. Now Cozens was to record for him those particular scenes to which he responded most deeply. Beckford owned a great many of J. R. Cozens' watercolours, including a sizeable group of views of lake Albano or lake Nemi, south of Rome. Both lakes have steeply rising banks, in places resembling cliffs, and both are the craters of extinct volcanoes. Above the precipitous side of lake Albano is sited Castelgandolfo, the summer residence of the Pope. These scenes were to inspire Beckford in creating Bitham lake at Fonthill.

In Naples again, Beckford renewed his friendship with the Hamiltons, though his stay was short, as Lady Hamilton became seriously ill. She died in August, and soon after Beckford returned to England. His ties with Sir William lasted however for many years, until Hamilton's death in 1803.

Beckford's marriage and subsequent difficulties in 1783–84 have already been mentioned. The Powderham scandal kept him out of England, and after his wife's death in 1786 he was to live abroad for much of the time until 1799, returning only for short visits of two or three months to Fonthill or London. He stayed again in Switzerland, and was in Paris during several episodes of the Revolution. His lengthiest stays were in Portugal, first from the spring of 1787 for several months, then in the '90s for periods totalling some three years. In July 1799 he returned to England, and was not to leave the country again apart from several short visits to Paris.

In this long time, his writings constantly reflect his fascination with nature and his love of gardens – linked with delight in the ecclesiastical architecture of the middle ages, from cathedrals to solitary hermit's cells. In Portugal, where he spent most time, his garden-making is uncertain, apart from his development of the 300-acre quinta at Monserrate, near Sintra, which he rented from the summer of 1794, and bought outright in 1798. Here he is supposed to have gardened greatly, and Gerald Luckhurst, who is now restoring the gardens for the municipality of Sintra, has shown me a ruined chapel, a rocky cascade and a primitive stone building which may all date from Beckford's period. The last of these bears a slight resemblance to the 'rude erection in imitation of a cromlech' at Fonthill. All three of these items at Monserrate are firmly in the 18th-century tradition of primitive, unsocial and wildly 'natural' features which we have already seen as part of the gardens at Painshill, Stourhead and the Fonthill of Alderman Beckford.

When Beckford left in 1799 Monserrate was neglected for many years. Byron, who visited Portugal in 1810, wrote of Monserrate as 'the most desolate mansion in the most beautiful spot I ever beheld' (letter of 25 September 1811 to R. C. Dallas), and in *Childe Harold* (canto I, pub. 1812, stanzas 22–23) he writes of the 'Paradise' which 'England's wealthiest son' once formed at Monserrate,

> But now, as if a thing unblest by Man
> Thy fairy dwelling is as lone as thou!
> Here giant weeds a passage scarce allow
> To halls deserted, portals gaping wide . . .

To return to Beckford. During his years abroad, English society continued to reject him, and several of his close acquaintances from the early 1780s were lost – Alexander Cozens, his wife Lady Margaret, his cousin Louisa, and Lady Hamilton had died, while others had grown away from him. Those about him, even the Chevalier Franchi, the master of his household, to whom he wrote countless letters, were always to some extent professionally attached, such as the architects, artists, gardeners, or agents for paintings or rare items of furniture with whom he was in contact while at work on the complex, many-dimensional creation of Fonthill Abbey and its surrounding domain.

*   *   *

As we have seen, the Alderman had made an ambitious garden landscape round his new house of Fonthill Splendens, with the great lake to the east, and numerous features in the surrounding estate. On his death in 1770, and during the following years of his son's minority, this landscape, like the house itself, will hardly have been neglected. But it is unlikely that any serious changes were made, and the last feature to be begun before his death, the projected tower on Stop's Beacon, was halted in its beginning. Splendens remained the centre, continuing to impress visitors with its combination of wealth and doubtful taste. As late as 1783, two years after William Beckford's coming of age, a visitor wrote: 'You would have been provok'd to see fine Titians pell mell with daubings of Casali . . . the mixture of good and bad pictures was hideous' (Mrs Boscawen, 25 September 1783, in *Life and Correspondence of Mrs Delany*, 1862, III, 141). Not that Beckford admired his father's house. He simply did not think of changing or replacing it – at least, not for many years. When, at last, in 1807, the main part of Splendens was demolished, Beckford wrote scathingly of 'this mass of very ordinary taste' (in Alexander, *op. cit.*, p. 42). In the meanwhile Splendens survived, and the earliest reference by Beckford himself to gardening activity at Fonthill (roughly parallel to his development of the 'Alpine garden', see below) is to do with an existing greenhouse at Splendens. Writing to his agent Thomas Wildman on 9 March 1787, he urges him to buy hothouse shrubs at a forthcoming auction: 'Let me enjoin you, as you love Fonthill and believe in the excellence of its conservatory, to buy fifty or a hundred pounds' worth of the grandest orange, oleander and myrtle trees' (in Alexander, *op. cit.*, p. 18).

The Alderman's gardens were therefore well maintained, and his son had begun to participate in their development. Beckford renewed contact with his early tutor, Robert Drysdale, in 1790, and in November 1791 Drysdale stayed for a while at Fonthill. On 1 November he wrote 'The walks are among the most beautiful in England and sixteen or seventeen or rather eighteen people are employed to keep them in good order continually' (in Oliver, *op. cit.*, p. 211).

The Alpine garden (in John Rutter, *Delineations of Fonthill*, 1823)

These 'walks' may have led from Splendens to viewpoints nearby, while some were probably part of the complex scheme of the 'Alpine garden' on the eastern side of Fonthill lake, which is first mentioned by a Dutch traveller, Baron van Spaen van Biljoen on 28 July 1791. He admired the 'large river' – Fonthill lake – and the 'fine waterfall' at its southern end. He adds:

> There are several grottoes cut in the living rock; to achieve this effect, very tasteful use has been made of the quarries which furnished the building materials for the house; the entrance to these grottoes is masked with creepers. There are also some artificial grottoes, a particularly fine one with a cold bath and another where the water peeping from the top was forming stalactites (H. Tromp, 'A Dutchman's visits to some English gardens in 1791', *Journal of Garden History*, II, 1, 1982, 48).

The 'artificial grottoes' were probably (as I have mentioned before) the features built in the Alderman's time. Close to these features however there is also a 50-yard tunnel, passing beneath the public road and leading into the grounds south of Splendens. Though this tunnel may likewise have been made for the Alderman, its purpose – to achieve privacy for visitors to the hermitage – and its rough and primitive character suggest that it may have been added for William Beckford.

The tunnel seems longer than it really is, since it changes direction half way, and its course is impeded by massy, rocky outcrops from walls, roof and floor. The darkness is intense. Such grotto tunnels, to pass privately under public roads, were common enough in the 18th century – Pope's Grotto at Twickenham is a well-known example. Beckford's tunnel near the hermitage is far more forbidding. Unlike the glittering, crystalline interior of Joseph Lane's grotto chamber at Painshill, this tunnel is harsh and gloomy, and has the oppressive atmosphere of a cavern sketched several times by J. R. Cozens in the Campagna in 1778. It does indeed appear to be 'cut in the living rock', as are sections of the grottoes along and above the eastern shore of the lake. From later accounts – Britton in 1801, Rutter in 1823, Redding in 1859 – we can piece together their origin and history.

The steep slope east of the lake had been quarried by the Alderman for stone needed for his new mansion. By about 1765 the main building work was complete, and so the quarry was 'thickly planted with firs'. This was to be the site of his son's Alpine garden.

Britton in 1801 lists many features in the Alpine garden which are not mentioned later. The whole area, wooded, and on sloping ground, was divided by paths, and opened up by lawns, to achieve 'successive contrasts between the lowest, the intermediate, and the highest ground'. The Alderman's bridge had gone in the 1780s, and visitors were now ferried across to the New Landing, to begin their tour 'through a wild walk'. Scenes included the Fairies' Lawn, 'surrounded by rising ground and rocky cliffs, clothed with hanging woods; the bottom enlivened with the gay vegetation of shrubs and flowers'; a 'wild quarry' (this is 'uncouth ground'); 'a root-house with a bowling-green in front, encircled with lofty firs, intermingled with lilac, woodbine, and laurel'; a viewpoint to see the mansion, 'from a ledge of rocks over which rises a moss-grown wall for the wanderer's safety whilst hanging on the precipice'; another viewpoint, of 'large pasture grounds, covered with flocks of sheep'; 'a rustic rotunda, called the Paliaro . . . thatched with straw . . . supported by six rude unbarked firs as columns', and then, 'striking down a savage path, screened on either side by thick, dark, and almost impenetrable wood, we arrive at a smooth level of green turf, on the top of a rock, where an urn or sarcophagus is to be placed, dedicated to the memory of Alexander Cozens . . . who was particularly partial to this spot' (Britton, *Beauties of Wiltshire*, I, 242–3). Cozens had died in 1786.

Beckford, wrote Britton, had 'managed' the whole 'so as to present to the moving spectator a continual variety of scenes, each marked with a different, and generally some striking character, calculated to inspire that particular sentiment, or emotion, intended in the plan'. This passage may well suggest that in the Alpine garden Beckford was trying to give form to that 'sentimental system of gardening' which Cozens had apparently described to him in 1777.

Within the continuing framework of lake, hillside and woodland, it would be hard to identify many of these features today. I do not know if a monument to Cozens was ever erected. The New Landing remains, later adorned with massive 19th-century urns, but another bridge, built in the early 20th century, has replaced the ferry. And the grottoes, first formed in the irregular holes, clefts and crannies, down and along the extent of Alderman Beckford's quarry, survive in chaotic, tumbled but convincing form.

They deserve separate comment, since they were the work of the dis-
tinguished maker of grottoes, Josiah Lane (1753–1833), son of Joseph
Lane, and since Beckford himself wrote about them at some length.
Lane Junior is credited with their execution, and Redding, from conver-
sations with Beckford in his old age, stated that the work was 'in imitation' of the grotto made at Painshill for Hamilton in the 1760s by Joseph
Lane. The words 'in imitation' are intriguing, since Hamilton's grotto
was both more glittering, more be-crystalled, and more compact than
the rambling labyrinth at Fonthill. What Josiah Lane achieved at
Fonthill ranks in extent and complexity with the elevated, cliff-edge
grottoes cut in the red sandstone for Sir Rowland Hill at Hawkstone in
Shropshire in the early 1780s. But here at Fonthill are no dizzying
views, but rather the mystery of a deeply shaded woodland approach,
with glimpses through the trees of dark caverns and rock archways to
one side, alternating with the sudden brightness of the lake on the
other.

Today, the woodland of this region is suitably wild, with pine and
yew, beech, oak and holly, undergrown with matted brambles and ivy.
But at the end of the 18th century these largely native growths were
variously enlivened – at suitable intervals – with patches of flowering
shrubs. Some of these are mentioned in Gilpin's and Britton's descriptions, and others listed more lavishly by Beckford himself, in his satirical
work *Modern Novel Writing, or the Elegant Enthusiast*: laurel, blossoming
thorn, lilac, guelder rose, laburnum, acacia and sweet-briar. These
plantings might indeed be a memory of his great-uncle's famous inno-
vations at Painshill. *Modern Novel Writing* (2v., 1796) was published
under the pseudonym 'Lady Harriet Marlow'. While much of the book
has nothing to do with gardens, part is a parody of the sentimental
romances of the time, including those of his half-sister Mrs Hervey. In
such novels, the grotto (wild) serves as a setting for episodes of fearful

suspense, and the grotto (picturesque) is the scene of gentler reflections, melancholy or romantic. In Beckford's novel (II, ch.6), he describes the park and gardens round Mahogany Castle, which could, in general terms, be the area between Splendens and Fonthill Lake – 'velvet lawn . . . pasture . . . a rising wood . . . river . . . immense park . . . groups of trees, with here and there a spire or a steeple peeping over their heads'. Then the reader is taken to 'Lord Mahogany's cave . . . the most delightful spot . . a terrestrial paradise'. The way passes through 'firs and forest trees', followed by the flowering shrubs, next 'darkened with the solemn gloom of cedars, and mournful cypresses'. Suddenly, we discover 'irregular steps cut in a rock', leading to 'the entrance of a spacious cave . . . hushed and silent, save that the trickling drops of a purling rill struck your ear'.

Beckford writes deliberately in the clichés of the sentimental novel – Peacock and Jane Austen will do the same in a few years' time. His phrases, then, are tongue in cheek; but he is also telling a good deal of truth, about his own, and Josiah Lane's creation. Britton's topographical patter is not dissimilar, for he says that Beckford's grotto is 'ornamented within by grotesque petrifactions, stalactites, madrepores, &c., aquatic plants and flowers shooting from the crevices. Its large interior space resounds with perennial springs trickling from various parts, and through channels here visible, and there unseen, hurrying along till lost in the waters of the lake'.

Britton omits however to mention one important feature of the 'large interior space', which Beckford describes, and which we may still admire today. Once inside 'Lord Mahogany's cave', 'a broken arch opened to your view the broad clear expanse of the lake, covered with numerous aquatic fowl, and weeping willows adorning the banks'. It is, in fact, like the grotto at Stourhead, and like the grotto at Painshill, endowed with the absolute delight of a view out across the lake, glimpsed privately, secretly through 'a broken arch', at the level of the water. Here, in his novel, Beckford allows Lord Mahogany to 'pass the sultry hours of the day' – like Beckford himself, or like Brooke Boothby in Wright of Derby's painting, he is 'stretched supinely on a bed of moss'. Here too, on his own, comes Lord Mahogany's son, Charles Oakley, to meditate upon 'the object of his flame'. 'Here he formed schemes of delusive joys, stifled the rising sigh, stopped the flowing tear, and . . . would often-times smoke a comfortable pipe, when the soft radiance of the moon played upon the pearly bosom of the adjacent waters'. Today, like the Boathouse far along the other side, this cavern has been affected by the slight rise in the level of the water, and Charles Oakley would now be wise to wear wellingtons. Yet the broken arch still reveals 'the broad clear expanse of the lake', and the size and roughness of the cave might allow a modern Beckford to imagine himself standing beside John Robert Cozens in 1778, while he sketched a cavern in the Campagna; or, in 1774, with Joseph Wright of Derby (when the guest of Sir William Hamilton) painting a grotto in the gulf of Salerno, and looking out at 'the pearly bosom of the adjacent waters'.

V

'Building Towers, Forming Gardens'

Beckford's Alpine garden, which he developed on the site of the quarry, was, like the walks at Splendens, still within the circuit of his father's ornamental park. He had however other, more individual ideas which were to be given a form, a reality far more grandiose, sublime and personal than the Alpine garden.

These ideas first appear in the late 1770s, and remain for years no more than fantasies – imaginative projects. From the start, they have three constant characteristics: there will be a tower, rising high above the garden and the outside world; the garden will be extensive and thickly wooded, and with a mountain or tall hill on which the tower is built; and the garden and its tower will be private, for the exclusive use of its master, and his few, most intimate friends. These objectives will never change – surviving the loss of Fonthill in 1822, to be re-interpreted at Bath in the next years, in the creation of Beckford's long, private ride up from Lansdown Crescent to Lansdown Tower.

The first expression of this idea is in a piece written by Beckford to Alexander Cozens in 1777–78. Beckford imagines that he will 'erect a tower dedicated to meditation'. The tower, approached by an avenue of trees, stands high 'on a lofty hill'. There, far above the world, they may 'survey the vast range of countries beneath', and feel themselves separate from, and superior to the common herd (in Alexander, *op. cit.*, pp. 153–6). The scenes he imagines are mostly nocturnal, lit by candles, stars or the moon – characteristic of his lifelong preference for scenes and moments experienced at sunset, in twilight, or in torch-illuminated darkness. Later in 1778, he visited the Grande Chartreuse, where, outside, he was constantly aware of the sublimity of the natural scene:

> I lifted up my eyes to the awful barrier of surrounding mountains, discovered by the trembling silver light of the moon . . . The lawns, the vast woods, the steep descents, the precipices, the torrents, lay all extended beneath, softened by a pale bluish haze . . . (in *Dreams, Waking Thoughts and Incidents*, pp.282, 287).

The images, and the ideal, often recur. In 1798 or '99, the second Lady Hamilton (née Emma Hart) looks back to a visit she had made to Fonthill, probably in late summer 1784, when Beckford had walked round with her talking of his ideas of 'great towers, little towers' and 'improvements' (*Hamilton and Nelson Papers*, letter 378). But the Powderham scandal had followed soon after, and with that, his most serious garden plans subsided until the 1790s.

He did not lack for means – in January 1790, following an improvement in the income from his sugar plantations, he wrote jubilantly to Lady Craven 'So I am growing rich, and mean to build Towers' (in Alexander, *op.cit.*, p.157) – and in the summer of 1791 he seems to have reached a decision to begin new work at Fonthill. Probably his idea was for a tower on Stop or Stop's Beacon, the wooded hill on the S.-W. side of the estate. On 23 June he wrote to Elizabeth Hervey of his love of Ossian, and of the proper place for enjoying such melancholy poems:

> I know not a place better calculated than Stops Beacon for northern gloomy writing. When I wander about the dark woods of pine . . . and when I discover between [the trees?] stretches of sky streaked with stormy red my imagination is crowded with the Heroes and phantoms of Fingal. I seem to hear shrill voices in the

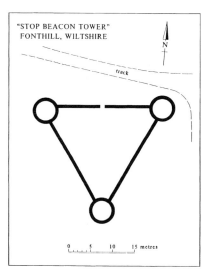

The plan of the Alderman's proposed tower,
on Stop or Stop's Beacon (Steven Ashley)

wind and my blood congeals as if by the approach of ghostly
beings (in Oliver, *op. cit.*, p. 210).

This solitary, elevated spot was where, in the late 1760s, his father had
begun to build a three-sided tower, in imitation of Henry Hoare's tower
at Stourhead. Now in 1791 William Beckford's chosen architect was
James Wyatt (1746–1813), who had already visited him at Fonthill in
1784. However, Wyatt was both dilatory and elusive, and he did not
supply designs for another two years. While Wyatt was to prove infuri-
atingly unreliable in this respect, Beckford was for his part often away in
the 1790s on the Continent. His negotiations with Wyatt – and with
other English contacts – were therefore protracted, and 'work', when it
began, was frequently undertaken in his absence.

At last, in the autumn of 1793, Beckford took the decisive step. He
ordered the building of a wall, to enclose 519 acres of the most elevated
part of his estate, lying a mile and more to the west and south-west of

Splendens, including Stop's Beacon some 2 miles south-west of the mansion. This wall was to be completed within a year, and to be twelve feet tall, surmounted by metal spikes – a *chevaux de frise*. With a winding course, the wall's initial length was about 8 miles, but it was extended to take in a total of some 1900 acres, with a circumference of about 12 miles. This was to incorporate part of a further 1700 acres added to his Fonthill estate (see *Hamilton & Nelson Papers*, letter 292, 2 February 1797). The wall had seven gates, the two most important being Stone Gate to the west, and the eastern gate reached from the outer drive leading through the park from the Beckford Arms. In the event, building took longer, and was probably complete by 1796 or 97. While Beckford's reasons for raising this wall are discussed later on, we must note that the area enclosed was emphatically remote from the original park and gardens of Splendens.

By the time the wall was complete, Beckford's schemes were under way. On 10 April 1794, Beckford had written to Wyatt about two building projects - one, for his residence in Portugal, to satisfy him temporarily, until the other – 'your magnificent plan for the Chapel upon Stop's Beacon' – could be executed (in Melville, *op. cit.*, p. 214). These projects didn't get very far, but in July 1796 Beckford's scheme reappears in a new and detailed form. It is outlined in a long entry on 20 July 1796 in the diary of the artist Joseph Farington, recording a conversation with his friend Wyatt that morning:

> Wyatt is going to Font Hill to Mr. Beckfords, who after an absence of 3 years, is lately returned to England. Wyatt shewed me the Plan and Elevation of a Tower, which He is going to build for Mr. Beckford. It is to be situated on a Hill, about 3 miles from Fonthill. At the foot it is to be 75 feet square. The height is to be 175 feet. The Story on which He is to live is to be 60 feet from the

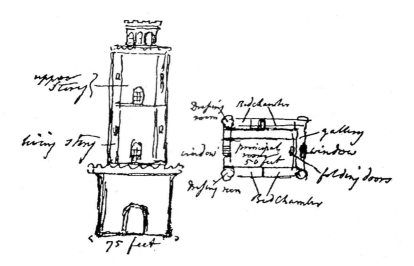

Farington's sketch of Wyatt's plan and elevation of a tower to be
built for William Beckford (*The Diary of Joseph Farington*,
ed. K. Garlick and A. Macintyre, II, 1978, 612. Reproduced by
gracious permission of H. M. the Queen)

ground . . . (*The Diary of Joseph Farington*, ed. K. Garlick and A.
Macintyre, II, 1978, 612).

While Farington's text shows Beckford retaining the site and approx-
imate size of the tower which Alderman Beckford had projected,
Farington also gives a sketch of the 'Plan and Elevation' of the tower,
taken from Wyatt's drawings. This sketch remains the first visual
record to survive of any of Beckford's ideas for a building at Fonthill,
and it takes the idea of the tower far away from the simple, rather gaunt
style of Alfred's Tower at Stourhead, which the Alderman had thought
to emulate. Instead, it has a striking resemblance to a building which
Beckford had often seen in Portugal, the Belem Tower at Lisbon. Completed in 1520 in exuberant late Gothic style, it has rounded corner
turrets, and prominent battlements shaped as the shields of the order of
the Knights of Christ.

The Belem tower, Lisbon (detail from Alexandre-Jean Noël's painting, c.1798)

It stands on an islet just off the northern shore of the Tagus estuary, a few hundred yards west of the convent of Belem. These topographical details are important, since they are positive indications that Beckford must have seen the tower many times – whenever he approached or left Lisbon by sea, and again when visiting the convent or driving past along the coastal road. The surviving journal of his first visit to Portugal begins on 25 May 1787 with 'We drove in the evening as usual along the sea shore by the venerable arches of the Convent of Belem' (*Journal . . . in Portugal and Spain* 1787–1788, ed. B. Alexander, 1954, p. 37); and we should note that leaving Lisbon by sea on 17 June 1796, the Belem Tower would have been the last object of architectural interest in Portugal to catch his eye.

Yet Beckford did not stay firmly with this idea. In the last quarter of 1796 his letters suggest that several designs, for two different sites, were being considered, and that one at least was partly executed. The chosen site was not Stop's Beacon, but Hinkley Hill, half a mile to the north-east – and still a mile west of Splendens. Here, most probably in the summer of 1796, work began on the 'convent', 'partly in ruins and partly perfect' (the terms used by Rutter in 1823), to embrace both the idea of an ancient monastic establishment, and Beckford's earlier, life-long wish for a tower. All this, I would add, develops within his new wall, and within an enclosing, living scheme of landscape. To Lettice he writes laconically on 5 Oct.1796 'the Convent advances – the walk extends' (in Melville, *op.cit.*, p.243), and to his mother, on 29 November1796 he writes in detail

> . . . I have extended the front of the Abbey in the Woods . . . to near two hundred feet, and a good part of the building has already reached the first floor. The Conservatory and flower Garden, which are to surround it, are begun. My Walk, which you will recollect is . . . to be carried considerably more than twenty miles thro' and round the Woods . . . has already proceeded to nearly the length of nine Miles. The Season proves admirable for my planting, and, if it continues as open till Christmas, I think Vincent ⌈his head gardener⌉ will by that time . . have got above a million of Trees into the Ground for this Year's work (ibid., pp.221–2).

'Chapel', 'ruined convent', 'tower', 'Abbey in the Woods' – this evolution in the architectural scheme continues, matched by development in the surrounding grounds. On 2 February 1798, Beckford writes to Sir William Hamilton 'I am staying my stomach with a little pleasure building in the shape of an abbey, which is already half finished. It contains appartments in the most gorgeous Gothic style . . . and a tower 145 feet high'. He adds 'I am not only building, but planting at a monstrous rate . . . The great drive, when finished, will extend, if you follow its various

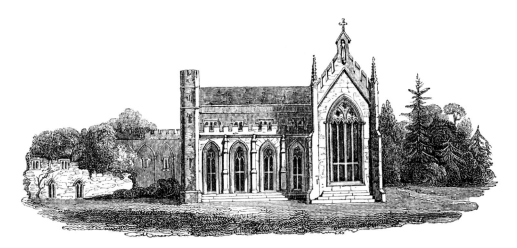

The Convent in Ruins (in John Rutter, *Delineations of Fonthill*, 1823)

windings, above thirty miles. How happy I should feel in once more guiding you and Ly. H. thro' this most singular labyrinth . . .' (*H. & N. Papers*, letter 292).

While the 'great drive' was now at its fullest extent – some 27 miles, through and round the great domain – the development of the building at the centre was to continue over many years. On 6 August 1797 Wyatt showed Farington his 'designs for Beckfords Gothic building – which is now much enlarged' (Farington, *Diary*, III, 880). By 6 November, Farington had heard that Beckford 'had an intention of taking down Fonthill House [i.e. Splendens] . . . and in that case enlarge the Gothic Building now erecting' and next day Wyatt added that 'the Spire of the new Gothic building is to be 300 feet high' (ibid., 916, 918). A year later (16 November 1798, ibid., 1091) Wyatt had yet more details, revealing that the project had been given its ultimate aesthetic and spiritual goal:

> New building to be called Fonthill Abbey – the Spire to be 17 feet higher than the top of St. Peters at Rome. – The Abbey to be endowed, and Cathedral Service to be performed . . . A Gallery . . .

to be decorated with paintings the work of English artists. – Beckford's *own tomb* to be placed at the end of this gallery.

From the 'Abbey in the Woods', it has finally become, and will remain, 'Fonthill Abbey'. Endowed, no, nor will Beckford's tomb ever be set within its Gothic walls – but the spire, the gallery – gallery upon gallery – were indeed to be built, rebuilt, altered and extended for the best part of twenty years. It remains a not-to-be-forgotten fact that for Beckford the Abbey, its contents, and its surrounding garden paradise were conceived as a unity, each part related to, and inseparable from the rest. I can think of only one other creation of such high importance which was conceived as a unified work, with linked architecture, décor and gardens – that is, the Château and gardens of Vaux-le-Vicomte, created, more or less from scratch, for Nicolas Fouquet between the mid-1650s and 1661. It is a rare occurrence. At Fonthill, the books – to put so rich an idea in a single word – represented wisdom; the paintings, jewels and sculpture provided beauty; the Abbey itself the shrine, and the gardens and grounds and woodland within the great wall were the natural setting for an aesthetic and spiritual whole.

So, in the last years of the 18th century, while the Abbey was taking shape, the surrounding park and woodland were developing with equal intensity. Most important was Beckford's creation of a large lake – Bitham or Bittern lake – a third of a mile south of the Abbey, and some 300 feet below the Abbey's site on Hinkley Hill. Like most garden lakes, it is artificial, with a firm dam put between two arms of the hillside, and a steeply falling slope beyond. Fed by a stream from the north-east, the overflow passes south.

What did this lake mean to Beckford? In 1812 Storer calls it 'a fine pellucid lake . . . in some parts of unfathomable depth, and having the appearance of the crater of an ancient volcano'. Storer may have been 'instructed' by Beckford when compiling his *Description*; but even without Storer's comment we are still able to see in Bitham lake a quiet, extinct volcano of the kind which J. R. Cozens drew in Italy many times in the 1780s, often in Beckford's company. Cozens' views are characteristically muted, melancholy, drawn and painted at the still moment of nightfall. If there are people in these pictures, they are small, set against the denseness of the woodland, the depth of the crater and the remoteness of the buildings on the further side.

Although Beckford's later letters add several telling points about Bitham lake, we do not know exactly when it was made. In the first edition of the 1″ Ordnance Survey map (sheet 15, pub. 1811), the wall is shown, the Abbey is marked 'Fonthill Abbey', but Bitham lake is not indicated. We know that surveys for the first edition, in southern England, were made in the late 1790s, and this suggests that, at the time of the Wiltshire survey, while the wall and the Abbey were there, Bitham lake did not yet exist. Set beside this are the drawings and paintings of Fonthill made by Turner in August / September 1799, now in the British Museum, in several of which Bitham lake appears in the foreground, with the Abbey on the high slope or skyline beyond. These facts may suggest therefore a date around 1798 for the creation of the lake – which would give reasonable time for Beckford to engage Turner to make his views of Fonthill.

Later, in 1817, Beckford himself indicates that he greatly enlarged the lake. In November 1817, 'a tremendous breach was opened in the great embankment. The water ran away rapidly' – and Beckford states that he will have to convert the area of the lake to meadows, 'or incur ruinous expense'. But he didn't want to do this, as it would destroy part of the 'noble features of Fonthill, especially after the sublime effect produced . . . by the particular shape I have given to the shore on a grand scale' (in Boyd Alexander, *Life at Fonthill* 1807–1822 (1957), p. 234,

Distant view of Fonthill Abbey (J. M. W. Turner, 1799)

letter of 8 November 1817). And so Bitham lake survives . . .

Another giant and artificial water-course from Beckford's time fol-
lows a tumbling line round the north-eastern side of Bitham lake, from
a higher source, and down to join the overflow from Bitham lake to the
south. This water-course, with frequent 'cascade' sections, winds down
within crude, massive yet carefully set blocks of stone, occasionally
stopped with cement, for no less than half a mile. No, it doesn't flow
today. But once, it was meant to, driven by a powerful hydraulic system,
and its rough, primitive or 'gothic' outlines fit wholly to the ideas of
Beckford – and Josiah Lane – in the late 1790s.

*   *   *

While visitors might inspect the principal rooms of Splendens from the
Alderman's day until at least the early 1800s, no such possibility existed

for viewing the Abbey until Beckford withdrew to Bath in 1822. Only once, in the last days of 1800, did Beckford ever hold a grand reception within its walls. The Abbey was still nowhere near complete, and Beckford had been obliged to hurry on the work to have sufficient rooms ready for his intended guests. As many as five hundred workmen were busy on the site at the same time, and work continued well into each night, illuminated by torches and lamps.

The reception was in several ways exceptional, and details should be related to show Beckford's ideas of the purpose of his Abbey and its grounds.

Early in November 1800, Lord Nelson, with Sir William and Lady Hamilton, returned to England from the Mediterranean. Since August 1798 Nelson, the Hero of the Nile, was everywhere welcomed as the saviour of the nation. He came in the company of the Hamiltons, as affairs of politics, love and war had brought him into frequent contact with them, and the court of Naples, in the previous two years. By now Lady Hamilton (who had been Emma Hart, and had married the widowed Sir William in 1791) had become Nelson's mistress. As Beckford commented, 'Lord Nelson's Lady Hamilton, or anybody else's Lady Hamilton', and so she, her husband and Nelson returned to England together. Just before Christmas 1800, they all came to stay as Beckford's guests at Fonthill.

They arrived from Salisbury at the great gatehouse by Fonthill lake to be greeted by an enthusiastic crowd, and the guard and band of the Fonthill volunteers. After cheering, and the playing of 'Rule Britannia', the volunteers 'marched on either side of the carriages' up to Splendens, where Beckford and his guests were waiting. More cheering, a feu de joie, 'God save the King'. The crowd of locals and the volunteers dispersed, while Beckford and his party entered the mansion.

The group included Beckford himself, Nelson, the Hamiltons, several

Nelson's visit – the nocturnal procession to the Abbey, 23 December 1800
(The *Gentleman's Magazine*, April 1801)

artists, many musicians, a few country neighbours, and several French émigrés. Not many from English society – the Powderham scandal in 1784 would never be forgotten. That evening – the 20th December – and for the following two afternoons and evenings the guests were entertained and accomodated at Splendens.

Not until the evening of the 23rd, at about 5 o'clock, when it was getting dark, was a visit made to the Abbey. Then a convoy of coaches collected the guests from Splendens, and at a slow pace set off through the grounds:

> . . . soon after having entered the great wall which incloses the abbey-woods, the procession passed a noble Gothic arch. At the point the company were supposed to enter the Abbot's domain; and hence, upon a road winding through thick woods of pine and fir, brightly illuminated by innumerable lamps hung in the trees, and by flambeaus moving with the carriages, they proceeded betwixt two divisions of the Fonthill volunteers, accompanied by their band playing solemn marches, the effect of which was much heightened by the continued roll of drums placed at different distances on the hills (*Gentleman's Magazine*, March 1801, 206–8).

The engraving in the *Gentleman's Magazine* catches the excitement. At the 'Gothic arch', no longer extant, the coaches roll on, lit by flaring torches, with the dark trees looming above. High up over trees, arch, coaches, riders and infantry, we glimpse a full moon, and the shadowy outline of the great, octagonal tower.

Arriving at the Abbey, the company were lavishly entertained. The main galleries were brilliantly lit, to show the costly fittings and works of art. Solemn music 'from some invisible quarter' followed, and then a collation in the library, and a series of dramatic 'attitudes' performed by Lady Hamilton. At 11 o'clock, 'delighted and charmed', they all left the

Abbey, and returned to the mansion-house (i.e. to Splendens) 'to sup'. 'On leaving this strange nocturnal scene . . . the company seemed, as soon as they had passed the sacred boundary of the great wall, as if waking from a dream, or just freed from the influence of some magic spell'. They slept at Splendens, and the next day left to go their different ways.

From the full account in the *Gentleman's Magazine*, it is clear that Beckford had done everything in his power to make it a sublime experience. His labours with the Abbey and its surrounding paradise were to continue for years, so that this already amazing creation was to become more and more rich, varied and wonderful. Yet the celebrations of December 1800 were never to be repeated, either by day or by night. Even in 1807, when Beckford at last took up residence in the Abbey, there was no 'grand opening', no 'house-warming'.

Wardour Castle and Fonthill Abbey (J. B. Knight, 1825 or earlier.
Courtesy of Salisbury and South Wiltshire Museum)

VI

'Twice Five Miles of Fertile Ground'

By the time of the entertainment for Lord Nelson in 1800, enough of the Abbey itself had been built, and enough of the surrounding gardens had been laid out to establish a scheme which was to remain much the same until Beckford left for Bath in 1822. When did he think to move to the Abbey, to live there? The idea must have have been in his mind for years, and with it the related intention of demolishing Splendens. In 1801, the connecting colonnades and passageways between the two pavilions and the main building were taken down. The decision to demolish the main building was taken in 1806, and in summer 1807 he moved at last to the Abbey, though building had still not finished. The last part, the eastern transept, was only partly completed in 1818. Major repairs are a continuing part of the Abbey's history.

By 1800, then, the essential scheme of Abbey and grounds had taken shape. What did this domain mean to Beckford? What were its characteristics?

Above all, it was a personal, and private creation. Splendens had not only an open site, but a 'public' background, derived from the Alderman's career. The Abbey and its grounds had therefore to be physically separate from Splendens and its gardens; to be different from all that Splendens had been; to express his, not the ideals of others; and to be a vehicle for his creative needs. All of which he had opportunity to achieve.

Much that is central to his purpose comes in a letter written in 1794 from Beckford to the Margravine of Anspach [i.e. his friend Lady Craven, who had married the Markgraf of Anspach in 1791]:

I cannot yet pretend to have taken the road of acquiring popularity, – for I have just stopped the career of fox hunters by a wall not quite so long or so high as that of China . . . I am extending my forests and sticking them full of hideous iron traps and spring guns that snap legs off as easily as Pinchbeck's patent snuffers snuff candles. In process of time, when my hills are completely blackened with Fir, I shall retreat into the centre of this gloomy circle like a spider into the midst of his web. There will I build my tower and deposit my books and my writings and brood over them . . . If I am shy or savage you must consider the baitings and worryings to which I allude – how I was treated in Portugal, in Spain, in France, in Switzerland, at home, abroad, in every region (in Oliver, *op. cit.*, pp. 257–8).

The letter is violent, exaggerated, mainly true. There is no more in his later letters of man-traps, but the wall, the misanthropy, the trees and the solitude will stay.

Most important is the wall. Begun in autumn '93, by '94 quite high enough to frustrate his trespassing neighbours, it was quickly known both for its extent, and for the secret nature of Beckford's life and building activities inside the forbidden enclosure. Already in 1801 the *Gentleman's Magazine* had written of 'the sacred boundary of the great wall', and in 1844, just after Beckford's death, Lansdown's account of Fonthill refers to 'the sacred enclosure' where 'a padlocked gate admits the visitor within the barrier' (*Recollections*, 1893, p. 40). As often as not, it is referred to by Beckford himself and by others as the 'barrier', the physical means of preserving his privacy, and keeping other people out.

At a simple level, he wished the building of the Abbey to proceed in a private way, and so, by 1800, while Splendens was still 'open to view', he was having to decline requests from strangers to inspect the Abbey and its grounds (Melville, *op.cit.*, pp.216–7). Several tales of 'intruders' are told. One of them, that related by Prince von Pückler-Muskau in a letter dated 23 Dec. 1828 is the most vivid:

> A neighbouring lord was so tormented by curiosity to see the estate that he set up a ladder against the high wall of the park one day, and climbed over. But he was soon discovered, and brought to Mr. Beckford. To his surprise, when he had explained who he was, Mr. Beckford received him very courteously, and for the whole morning conducted him round in person, gave him a splendid lunch, and then at last withdrew, bidding his visitor farewell with the greatest respect.
>
> Delighted with the outcome, the visitor now wanted to go home, but he found all the gates were closed, and no one there to open them. He was forced to return to the Abbey to ask for help; and there he was told, 'Mr. Beckford will kindly permit you to leave by the way you came in. The ladder remains where you left it.' The lord protested, but in vain, and he was obliged to seek out the spot where he had broken in to the estate and clamber up the ladder again. Cursing the malicious misanthropist, and cured for ever of the desire to visit Fonthill, he left the forbidden Paradise (in *Briefe eines Verstorbenen*, 1836, I, ii, 292–5. Tr. C.T.).

Who was this 'neighbouring lord'? The story reads better as myth than fact. But one 'neighbouring lord' did indeed penetrate the forbidden domain – Sir Richard Colt Hoare, from nearby Stourhead. Though Beckford's neighbour, and contemporary (he was born in 1758, Beckford in 1760), they seem to have met rarely, and since the Powderham scandal in 1784 acquaintance with Beckford was frowned on. But by 1806 Sir Richard was compelled to write to Beckford for permission to visit Fonthill, for his research in preparing the *History of Modern Wiltshire*. The story is told both by Farington (*Diary*, 16 October 1806) and by Redding (*op.cit.*, II, 142–4). Beckford replied, granting the request, but to avoid embarassment Sir Richard came at a time when he thought Beckford would be away.

> He spent some hours in taking notes upon . . . the Abbey and grounds . . . Just as he was leaving, a servant requested him to step into one of the rooms he had not yet seen, and upon entering it he saw Mr.Beckford himself, and the table laid out for a repast. Sir Richard was never more surprised in his life . . .

The two 'spent the evening very agreeably'. Beckford said after (to Redding) 'You never saw a poor man so much astonished as when I suddenly pounced upon him. Had I been a whole Gorgon, he could not have been more petrified'.

But the meeting had sad results. Sir Richard was attacked by 'neighbouring gentlemen who took such umbrage at it' that he was asked to explain his conduct. He replied (to the Marquess of Bath) that 'he had no further desire but to see the Abbey and the meeting with Mr. Beckford was accidental', while on his side Beckford confided to Wyatt that Sir Richard 'while looking over the Abbey made some good observations but He afterward sd. "Sir Richard had no taste".' They do not seem to have met again.

Beckford himself writes in near-hysterical terms about the invasion of privacy. To Franchi he exclaims 'Blessed abbey, save and defend me from such riff-raff and riff-raffery as this! Grow, you forests, raise yourselves, you walls, and make an everlasting barrier between me and them' (24 October 1811, in Alexander, *op.cit.*, p.109). Four years later, on 17

September 1815, he writes 'The craze for seeing the Abbey grows like the Tower itself – every day and well-nigh every hour they [would-be visitors] twist and turn to corrupt my dragoons – so far in vain' (ibid., p. 183).

We might note, as a secondary effect of his desire to exclude the world, the vaunted tameness of the birds and animals in the grounds. When, in 1817, Samuel Rogers visited the Abbey, he said that he and Beckford 'were met at the setting out by a flock of tame hares, that Mr. Beckford feeds; then Pheasants, then partridges' (in Brockman, *op.cit.*, p. 169).

*   *   *

Within the wall, Beckford's garden creation was independent, and his own. A couple of phrases, from Rutter (1823) and Redding (1859), indicate how important this work was to him. Having said to Redding that the Abbey was 'the great work of his life' (Redding, *op.cit.*, II, 146), we should note that the grounds were 'constructed upon one pervading principle of art' (Rutter, *op.cit.*, p. 92). This explains totally Beckford's rejection in July 1799 of Humphry Repton's offer 'to contribute to the ornament' of Fonthill (in Melville, *op.cit.*, p. 256). There are no details. Beckford was engaged in a wholly personal creation, in which the help – or intrusion – of others would be wrong. By the 1790s he had yearned, dreamed of his ideal landscape for so long that it was in fact pointless for anyone else to suggest that they might 'landscape' his domain for him.

The area within the wall was intensely private, so much so that work on the grounds was often carried out at night, that Beckford might not have his mood disturbed by the presence of teams of gardeners. In particular the mowing of grass along the main avenues – such as the mile-long Great Western Avenue from Stone Gate to the west front of the

Abbey – was nocturnal. (It is proper to add that this was done with scythes, much easier in the half-light than a rotary mower, which had in any case not yet been invented!) Most of the time, year after year, the grounds were enjoyed by Beckford on his own. So great was the extent of his personal paradise that he must have felt little external restraint; and when, from the Abbey tower, he looked out over his domain and the surrounding lands, he would have known his solitary superiority to the full. Round his own land, the Wiltshire countryside was 'a vast desert plain', and so the few details of further landmarks that were discernible were as if in other kingdoms – the romantically ruined castle at Wardour; the gothic turrets of Alfred's Tower at Stourhead; the slender, medieval Cathedral spire at Salisbury. His tower at Fonthill must have been visible from a distance of many miles – mysterious, inaccesible, like its owner. The view by J. B. Knight, *Wardour Castle and Fonthill Abbey* (painted in the 1820s, now in the Salisbury and South Wiltshire Museum) gives a fine impression of this Gothic marvel, gigantic on the distant skyline, densely surrounded and protected by millions of trees.

The solitary view from his tower may recall the fantasy he elaborated in *The Vision* (see p. 66 above); yet that was imagined in the company of his cherished mentor Alexander Cozens. By 1786 Cozens was dead, and Beckford's other intimate friends were scattered. We have no idea of how he, the unique metteur-en-scène of the Christmas 1800 festivities, felt at the end of the affair. Beckford was no stranger to nocturnal solitude – this his letters show. But we should remember the convivial, twilight lakeside parties in Switzerland – 'it may be the happiest day of my life', he had then declared.

*   *   *

Beckford's ideal was of the total landscape, enjoyed as a solitary, dream-like experience, untroubled by tedious companions, and proceeding, without concern, through the varied scenes nature provides. There is little change in his relationship to nature, though the terms become more perceptive as he grows older. To Alexander Cozens he writes, aged 19, on 13 March 1779, 'I am become wild and timid as a stag, long used to roam in the recesses of the forest. I start when a Frangui [a stranger] presents himself, and, plunging into my solitudes, remain silent and fearful, till he is gone out of my sight. The news of the World affects me not half so much as the chirping of a sparrow, or the rustling of withered leaves' (in Melville, *op. cit.*, p. 83).

A year later, in the Tyrol, he slips away from his companions to make his way along a goat-track, finding a cascade. There, the sunset light on the splashing, falling water 'diffused a repose, a divine calm, over this deep retirement, which inclined me to imagine it the extremity of the earth, and the portal of some other region of existence . . . I hung eagerly on the gulph, impressed with this idea, and fancied myself listening to a voice that bubbled up with the waters; then looked into the abyss and strained my eyes to penetrate its gloom, but all was dark and unfathomable as futurity! Awakening from my reverie, I felt the damps of the water chill my forehead . . .' (26 July 1780, *Dreams, Waking Thoughts and Incidents*, pp. 143–4).

Returned to Fonthill, he writes to his cousin Louisa Beckford 'the gleam of a setting sun is the very light to pine by. A mournful species of enthusiasm often drives me at this hour to the vast desert plain which stretches out beyond our little woody region of Fonthill' (14 July 1781, in Oliver, *op. cit.*, p. 72).

Best content on his own, 'conversing' with nature, uneasy in company, yet relating his feelings in letters, Beckford's attitude will barely change. It is related to – one might say partly derived from – that of Rousseau, whose *Nouvelle Héloïse* (1760) and *Émile* (1762) describe the solitary 'natural' garden, the 'Élysée', where a visitor may enter only by permission of the virtuous heroine (these groves belong to birds, and nature, not to man), and the solitary education of Émile, a boy brought up away from society (and his parents) and taught not by man, but by nature. Beckford owned these works in several editions, and also owned the *Rêveries*, first published in 1782.

Sad, yet most revealing, is his journey in June 1786, after the death of his wife in Switzerland. Lettice, his old tutor and friend, proposed an excursion to parts he had not seen before, and they went to the lac de Bienne. There, at the île Saint-Pierre – the setting for the most poetic and nature-centred of Rousseau's *Rêveries* – Beckford confessed 'the soothing power of the change . . . so that he felt amid the new and fascinating scenery, something at times "which stole him from himself"' (Redding, *op. cit.*, I, 273).

Rousseau began the *Rêveries* with the declaration of his spiritual and social solitude: 'So now I am alone on the face of the earth, having no brother, neighbour, friend or company apart from myself'. Beckford might have echoed this, at the île Saint-Pierre in 1786. Later in the *Memoirs* (II, 350) Redding records that Beckford told him of his life-long passion for solitude, which he linked with his love of nature, and of the Alps: 'I lived in Switzerland among the Alps, at twenty-six, under a bitter domestic calamity. I found their solitude soothed me as nothing else would – I have loved solitude more since.'

Beckford's Fonthill domain was indeed similar in spirit to Julie's 'Élysée' in the *Nouvelle Héloïse*. Beckford, like Saint-Preux, visits his gardens as a promeneur solitaire, drawing strength and solace from nature like Anson's storm-battered sailors on the uninhabited island of Tinian. In his feelings for nature (if in little else!) Beckford writes and acts singularly like a Rousseau who has achieved independence through wealth. Shunned by man, he can still create a lavish natural solitude.

At Fonthill Beckford was, therefore, profoundly alone for much of the time, as solitary as a hermit, with a hermitage the size of a cathedral. His garden, grounds, park and woodland never had a fixed itinerary, since spontaneity, the quality of 'naturalness', was essential. With himself the sole traveller along the miles of paths, they were left un-gravelled, grassy as a woodland track. When Rutter compiled his *Delineations of Fonthill* in 1823, his text was for a public which had never been allowed to enter the estate, for strangers who now came in their hundreds, permitted as possible purchasers, to marvel and to explore. Describing the grounds 'within the barrier', he writes at one point: 'When we first visited this charming path, it was almost unknown, and we delighted to wander

> O'er the smooth enamell'd green,
> Where no print of step hath been.

It has now been explored by unnumbered visitors, but it is still fresh and beautiful; and the elastic moss seems still to have been only trodden by its native tenants, the thousands of fearless hares and rabbits, that the kindness of the late proprietor encouraged about his domain' (*Delineations*, p. 85).

No set route; no gravelled paths; few garden buildings. What need was there, when, most often, only Beckford himself was passing from scene to scene? Beside the Norwegian Lawn (west of Stop's Beacon) there was the Norwegian Hut – 'a sort of log house, of very tasteful pro-portions' (ibid., p. 91) – and there were lodges, for gatekeepers, and to serve as 'occasional shelter'. These are all the garden buildings Rutter describes, apart from the Alderman's boathouse, and the grottoes by Fonthill lake. Storer in 1812 had not mentioned any others, nor did Loudon in 1835, looking back to a visit he made in 1807. But they men-tion other aspects of the domain – Storer writes of the 'Chinese Garden, particularly appropriated to the culture of the rarest flowers', and

The Norwegian hut – 'a block house of a tasteful character'
(in John Rutter, *Delineations of Fonthill*, 1823)

Loudon mentions a similar 'small flower-garden', in an angle of the Abbey, a herb garden 'containing such plants as we may suppose the monks might have collected to use in medicine', and a garden 'for a favourite dwarf', with 'a small hot-house in it, not much bigger than a cucumber frame' (*Gardener's Magazine*, XI, Sep. 1835, 444). The dwarf would have been Pierre (or Perro, or Pierrot, and sometimes 'Nanibus') de Grailly, who came from Evian, and was with Beckford from 1788 until his death in 1828.

The rest is trees. Innumerable conifers, native deciduous trees, and areas of special kinds – 'a rose-ground, a thornery, and a pinetum' (ibid., 443) carefully hidden away among the native species. Beside the Abbey, only two exotic trees were visible, 'an apricot and a fig tree, planted against the south side of the grand entrance, as we may suppose by some monk who brought the seeds of these fruits from some Italian or Swiss monastery' (ibid., 442). Down by Bitham lake, on its eastern side, was the American plantation, 'broken into picturesque forms by the margin of the water', and vivid with 'every variety of the magnolia, azalea, and rhododendron hitherto imported'. Elsewhere, a mile-long path was 'bordered with the scarlet thorn . . . and variegated hollies' (Storer, in Melville, *op.cit.*, pp. 356-7).

His principal gardeners – Vincent, from 1796 until Beckford's death in 1844, and Milne, who left his service in 1815 – were both intelligent and trusted employees (Milne was a minor botanist, corresponding with Sir James Smith), and Vincent was consulted daily on garden matters, both at Fonthill and later in Bath. Yet they remained employees, and he the master. Virtually without friends, Beckford traversed his paradise alone.

But he had still to write down his experiences, as he had done, long before, to Alexander Cozens. His letters to Franchi, his secretary, tell

'A View at Fonthill Abbey'.
Beckford's dwarf, Pierre de Grailly, seen in front of Bitham lake
(in John Britton, *Graphical and Literary Illustrations
of Fonthill*, 1823)

The American plantation (in John Rutter, *Delineations of Fonthill*, 1823)

much of his life at the Abbey: discomfort, frustration, irregular consultations with Wyatt; contacts with dealers in London, news of the big world, and the rare visitor, such as 'Father' Smith, the painter; and, from time to time, the glory of his garden-creation. One letter, on 18 December 1818, confirms this achievement:

I went with the Father himself . . . in those oakwoods which are so like Genzano [near lake Nemi] and even at moments Cintra. The softest and most luminous vapours covered a landscape that might have been Italian: the hills transformed into mountains and the valleys into lakes produced a thousand illusions . . . a boundless sea, varied, however, by splendid shores, with here and there little wooded islands clad in the gayest green . . . All the Abbey forests were enamelled by a lurid sun under the loveliest blue sky, and from out of these forests rose the Castle of Atlas with all its windows sparkling like diamonds! Nothing I've ever seen in my life can equal this unique vision in grandeur of form or magic of colour

... They talk of the mirage in Egypt and in the great desert: I have now seen it, and seen it at Fonthill (in Alexander, *op. cit.*, p. 260).

*　　*　　*

After the demolition of the central block of Splendens, one of the two flanking pavilions was taken down in 1811. Beckford, residing in the Abbey in solitary and often uncomfortable splendour, thought at one point to adapt the remaining pavilion of Splendens as a winter residence. Though this plan wasn't carried out, the pavilion was allowed to stand, and it was indeed to become the residence for part of the divided estate in 1826.

Already in 1811 Beckford had found his wealth to be finite. The price of sugar had dropped, and his agents in Jamaica were less than honest. Yet his building or rebuilding of the Abbey went on, as did his buying of rare books and paintings. So something had to be sold. First, his estates outside Fonthill were given up – in 1811, the estate of Witham Priory, north of Stourhead, was sold (see Alexander, *op. cit.*, p. 92, n. 4). A while later, Fonthill itself was affected, as he began to fell one area of woodland after another. Some may have been planted by the Alderman, but much more may have been 20-year growth from his own plantings in the 1790s. While in 1814 he might still be re-planting as he felled, he had within a few years sold most of his remaining mature timber, and the continued thinning of the trees began to threaten the quality of his landscape. By 1819, both the shores of Bitham lake, and the woodland overlooking the site of Splendens were threatened – but, as he wrote to Franchi on 2 Oct. 1819, 'I have no other resource, as you well know' (ibid., p. 319).

For a while in 1816 he toyed with the idea of making 'a kind of farm in the very interior of the sacred Enclosure', and with this in mind, in May 1817 he came close to draining Bitham lake to make it into mead-

Visitors ticket to Fonthill Abbey, 1823 (John Stedman Whitwell)

ows (ibid., pp. 195, 203). But the struggle was too great. By September 1817 he thinks that he will 'shut up shop' at Fonthill. From time to time his gardens bring him deep delight, but his growing debts force him to sell. The visitors, excluded for so long, arrive in their hundreds, armed with Christie's catalogue of the contents to be sold at auction. The sale, first set for 17 September 1822, was postponed, then cancelled, when John Farquhar, a millionaire as eccentric as Beckford himself (though in different ways. Beckford referred to him as 'Old Filthyman') bought the entire estate, the Abbey, and its fixtures on 5 Oct. 1822 for £300,000.

Beckford moved to Bath, to Lansdown Crescent, acquiring two houses which he connected by a bridge. Again he gardened, developing a long, winding strip of land leading uphill for one and a quarter miles to Lansdown Hill. There, in 1825–6, he built another tower, and his remaining years (he did not die until May 1844) were spent between the houses, the garden-ride, and Lansdown Tower. Near the foot of the tower is his tomb.

VII

'Partly in Ruins and Partly Perfect'

In 1846 (curiously close to Beckford's death) Edgar Allan Poe wrote a short tale, *The Domain of Arnheim*, first published in March 1847 in the *Colombian . . . Magazine.* This tale relates the quest of one Ellison, who on his 21st birthday inherited the largest private fortune the world had ever known. What should he do with it? 'In the widest and noblest sense, he was a poet' – and so it seemed to him 'that the creation of the landscape-garden offered to the proper Muse the most magnificent of opportunities'. The rest of his life and his fortune are then devoted to the search for a site – the domain of Arnheim – and the creation of this supreme work of art. Here, we should note that the narrator proposes only one comparison between Ellison's achievement, and earlier gardens. The comparison is made with Fonthill – for just as Ellison's greatest-of-all-fortunes is devoted to Arnheim, so Beckford gave his immense wealth in creating the work of art that was Fonthill.

∗   ∗   ∗

Beckford left Fonthill in 1822. In December 1825 the central tower of the Abbey collapsed, destroying a fair part of the building in its fall. In 1826, the estate was divided into three lots, and has remained in divided ownership.

By 1829, in vol.V of the *History of Modern Wiltshire*, Sir Richard Colt Hoare could entitle the engraving of the ruined Abbey 'Fonthill eheu! dilapsus', and within a few years the great fabric had been reduced to no more than the northern tip, a fragment which still survives – so small that it looks like a tiny parish church. To the south a spacious area of lawn marks where the main body of the Abbey had been. According to Rutter the 'intended structure' which Beckford had first envisaged in the 1790s was to have been 'a Convent, partly in ruins and partly perfect'. It is indeed curious how closely the remaining portions of the Abbey have come to resemble his original idea . . .

Meanwhile the last pavilion of Splendens – which Sir Richard Colt Hoare had cheerily entitled *Fonthill resurgens* – had also dwindled, the last of it being demolished in the mid-20th century. Another mansion – also named, confusingly, Fonthill Abbey – had been built in 1848–52, roughly midway between the sites of Splendens and the Abbey. This too was blown up in 1955, leaving only its formal terraces, with sculptures, and a group of stable buildings to be re-developed from 1978 onwards. Amid this decline, in a divided estate, the garden features were neglected or destroyed. The great circling wall remains in a few, shattered stretches, rarely more than 4' or 5' tall, and the other items which may be found – whether from the Alderman's or from William Beckford's time – are alike in their dilapidation. Only the great gateway, built in the 1750s over the public road, subsists in its entirety. But its purpose, to announce the imminent grandeur of Splendens, has gone.

Painshill endured a similar, but less brutal decline. Benjamin Bond Hopkins, who bought the property in 1773, had a new mansion built between 1775 and '78, south of Hamilton's house. Visits to the gardens continued unabated until the turn of the century.

Stourhead was the least affected by such changes. Remaining in the Hoare family, the estate was managed with reasonable continuity throughout the 19th century. The character of the gardens was however profoundly altered by the introduction of new and unfamiliar trees and shrubs (their details are carefully recorded in the 'Annals of Stourhead',

Detail from Martin's view of Fonthill Abbey,
from Storer, *A Description of Fonthill Abbey*, 1812. The sanctuary
and the small Lancaster tower on the left hand side are
all that now remain

maintained from 1792 to 1860, and from 1894 to 1947. See Woodbridge, *The Stourhead Landscape*, pp. 35, 64–70). These new species have added dimensions, colours and emphasis which Henry Hoare could not have imagined.

*　　*　　*

I have often visited these three gardens, questioning 'how they would have been'. It is also fair to ask – or at least to wonder – what their makers would think of them today.

Henry Hoare, a diligent and serious man, recommending a conscientious way of life as the prerequisite of happy garden-making, might reasonably be satisfied. His experience of bereavement might school him to accept his family's departure from Stourhead, while the continuing and thoughtful care of the National Trust since 1946 would certainly match his demand for responsibility. His sociable side would have acknowledged the public eagerness to view, and admire, his and his grandson's creation, and to enjoy musical performances, and firework displays, held by the lake at Stourhead in recent years.

Hamilton too would not be displeased. Forced to sell Painshill when his garden was at its point of perfection, he did not live to see its decline. To return today, with a restoration scheme in splendid progress since 1981 (in that year the Painshill Park Trust was formed, after purchase of 158 acres of the original estate), he would find his lake, his monuments and follies, and his planting schemes the object both of study and restoration. As in his own day, no house impinges on the landscape. He would, I think, be pleased yet surprised at the lavish repairs to his Gothic temple, the grotto, the mausoleum and other features (the Turkish tent has been completely recreated), and he would be gratified at the interest shown in his choice of trees, and his possible schemes of planting.

At Fonthill, the Alderman might simply walk away, to find a better place; or, who knows, pull out his pocket book, and calculate the cost of another garden, beside another Splendens, both bigger and grander than before.

And his son, William Beckford? He too, like Hamilton, left because he could not afford to stay. The estate was sold, the Abbey fell down, the estate was sold again, and divided, and the parts have since been farmed, or forested,with scant thought to their past share of paradise.

No doubt, he would think poorly of the public throng at Stourhead; he might smile wryly at Stourhead's and Painshill's present fame. But what might his feelings be, revisiting his own Fonthill, still with the lakes he and his father made, still forested, yet abbeyless, divided, the long rambling grottoes tumbled and overgrown?

I like to think that he, William Beckford, far more than Hamilton or Hoare, with the gardens they had made, would find this shattered Fonthill still true to his desire. A ghost himself, he could pace the empty lawn, site of the Abbey, and dream again of towers; looking at what remains – barely the size of a chapel – he could revel undisturbed in Ozymandian despair, and then, as long before (day after day, for year after year) he could make his way unseen along those miles of winding paths, along the great terrace with views out over half the world, and down through densely planted woods to reach the silent crater-lake. Here, alone and unperceived, himself the hermit, most solitary of all, he could brood for hours on end, his thoughts with the sunset, or far away in eastern fantasy, or joined once more in happy converse with long-dead friends.

Fonthill remains a private wilderness, an Eden where *rêverie* is always possible, Bitham lake still mingling with lake Albano, the wooded Alpine slopes still enclosing the ghostly hermit's cell, ruined convent, tower, and at last the Abbey – an ideal of paradise pursued to its earthly uttermost.

A Brief Bibliography

Painshill

Hodges, Alison, 'Painshill Park, Cobham, Surrey', *Garden History*, II, 1
    (Autumn 1973), 39–68

Hodges, Alison, 'Painshill, Cobham, Surrey: the Grotto', *Garden History*, III, 2
    (Spring 1975), 23-28

Kitz, Norman & Beryl, *Pains Hill Park*, 1984

Stourhead

Woodbridge, Kenneth, *Landscape and Antiquity: Aspects of English Culture at
    Stourhead 1718 to 1838*, 1970

Woodbridge, Kenneth, *The Stourhead Landscape*, 1986

Fonthill

Alexander, Boyd, *England's Wealthiest Son*, 1962

Alexander, Boyd, ed., *Life at Fonthill 1807–1822*, 1957

Berry, Julian, ed., *William Beckford Exhibition 1976*, 1976

Brockman, H.A.N., *The Caliph of Fonthill*, 1956

Lees-Milne, James, *William Beckford*, 1976

Melville, Lewis, *Life and Letters of William Beckford*, 1910

Morrison, A., ed., *Hamilton and Nelson Papers*, 2v., 1893–94

Oliver, J.W., *The Life of William Beckford*, 1932, 1937

Redding, Cyrus, *Memoirs of William Beckford of Fonthill*, 2v., 1859

Rutter, John, *Delineations of Fonthill and its Abbey*, 1823 (facsimile 1972)

Storer, James, *A Description of Fonthill Abbey*, 1812

Grottoes

Thacker, C., *Masters of the Grotto: Joseph and Josiah Lane*, 1976

General

Thacker, C., *The Genius of Gardening: the History of Gardens in Britain and
   Ireland*, 1994

Index